LIFE IN THE SPIRIT

JOHN WESTON

Energion Publications
Gonzalez, FL
2017

ISBN10: 1-63199-436-0
ISBN13: 978-1-63199-436-4
Library of Congress Control Number:

Energion Publications
P. O. Box 841
Gonzalez, FL 32560
energionpubs.com
pubs@energion.com
850-525-3916

ACKNOWLEDGEMENTS

I would like to thank my daughter Elizabeth for her hard work in compiling this book of my study into the Beatitudes and the Holy Spirit. My beautiful wife, who is my greatest support and love of my life. The prayers and support of my church family at Harmony Baptist Church in Semmes, Alabama.

Most of all I give all the glory to my Lord and Savior Jesus Christ.

TABLE OF CONTENTS

INTRODUCTION

The topic of this study is based on observations within the church in general and scriptural reflections in opposition to those observations. There are many negative understandings and teachings concerning the Holy Spirit and His work among Believers. The many different responses, in most congregational settings, range from a paranormal, supernatural fear to the rejection of the Holy Spirit even existing. Another theological stand is that the Holy Spirit was only present with Jesus Christ Himself. Just the mere thought of the notion of a spirit living within a person made even those who call themselves "born again" Christians tremble in fear of "possession." These are common misunderstandings rooted in much of the watered-down Christianity of today. The most common belief is that the Holy Spirit is God's Spirit and is not to be spoken of at all. How does a person grow in Christ if not through the work and power of the Holy Spirit?

The idea for this study on the Holy Spirit was inspired by God because of the total misconceptions and misunderstandings found prevalent within the Body of Christ, the church. Jesus taught His disciples concerning the Spirit. He said that soon He would be leaving and He would send the "Comforter" which is the Spirit of God to be the guide for all who believe.

From the beginning, Jesus taught His disciples the way to the abundant life and beyond into eternity. The attitude and character of someone entirely focused on God alone. In the Sermon on the Mount, Matthew chapters five through seven, Jesus taught specifically to this understanding. The following chapters, until His death and resurrection, were examples that demonstrated the power of God and His Spirit through the ministry of the Son. Jesus outlined for His disciples eight character attitudes for the Believer to strive to achieve. It was not until the disciples received that same Holy

Spirit in the upper room on the day of Pentecost that they truly began to allow the Spirit of God to empower them. These first eight statements of Godly character were to be the foundation and later building blocks for lives incredibly formed.

The Holy Spirit empowers Believers for God's Holy vision and mission to save His creation and reconcile them back to Himself. When the Holy Spirit came into the lives of humanity, the final era of reconciliation began and continues until Jesus' return. In Matthew Chapter Five, Jesus teaches eight basic attributes that a true Believer in Jesus Christ should, in the process toward sanctification, exhibit and live as a light in a world of darkness.

Blessed are the poor in spirit,
For theirs is the kingdom of heaven.

Blessed are those who mourn,
For they shall be comforted.
Blessed are the meek,
For they shall inherit the earth.
Blessed are those who hunger and thirst for righteousness,
For they shall be filled.
Blessed are the merciful,
For they shall obtain mercy.
Blessed are the pure in heart,
For they shall see God.
Blessed are the peacemakers,
For they shall be called sons of God.
Blessed are those who are persecuted for righteousness' sake,
For theirs is the kingdom of heaven.

Blessed are you when they revile and persecute you, and say all
kinds of evil against you falsely for My sake. Rejoice and be
exceedingly glad, for great is your reward in heaven, for so they
persecuted the prophets who were before you. (Matthew 5:3-14)

The Beatitudes, as they have been later known, the guiding path set before every disciple of Jesus Christ, since the beginning of His ministry. Jesus demonstrated each one in everyday life experiences. However, He also made known to the disciples that it is the Spirit of God that guides the true Believer into a right and focused intimate relationship with Him. Being able to understand the roles of the Trinity in the life of the individual Believer will assist the one seeking that perfect relationship with God. Through this relationship, one can strive with others for the work of the eternal Kingdom of God.

The Believer should be made aware of the power that the Holy Spirit brings when allowed to work in their life. God gives the true Believer power and authority over the things of the world. Knowing that Jesus sent the Holy Spirit, as a gift for each of us to use for the glory of God, should be inspiration enough to strive for that closer relationship. Their desire should be first and foremost for God the Father, God the Son and God the Holy Spirit. This is the total package for the Believer. There is no belief in one or two and exclude the other. So, reach deep into your spirit and connect with the teachings of Jesus Christ in the scriptures concerning God's Spirit and His work. It is a work that thrives within the life of the Believer who strives and desires to grow in Spirit and in Truth and to lead a life truly glorifying to God.

1

The Role of the Holy Spirit

And it shall come to pass afterward
that I will pour out My Spirit on all flesh;
your sons and your daughters shall prophesy,
your old men shall dream dreams,
your young men shall see visions.
And also on My menservants and on My maidservants
I will pour out My Spirit in those days.   (Joel 2:28-29)

The Spirit of God, or the Holy Spirit, is the same Spirit present at the creation of all things. He is the same Spirit that spoke to Moses on Mount Sinai. This Spirit of God is the same Spirit that came down from heaven in the form of a dove and rested upon the person of Jesus the Christ in preparation for His ministry. He is the same Spirit that fell upon those in the upper room on the day of Pentecost in Acts Chapter Two.

The Apostle Paul, in his letter to the Ephesian church, spoke pointedly out of concern for their misunderstanding of the role of the Spirit in the individual. When the Apostle John wrote concerning the logos or word in the first chapter of his gospel, it was all inclusive since creation. When God created all things, the God that was mentioned is the God of the Trinity, Father, Son, and Holy Spirit. If we truly believe in God the Father and God the Son, then God the Holy Spirit is just as credible. The modern-day church, particularly mainline denominations, become more institutionalized and develop into legalized religious organizations. Many times,

I have spoken in meetings and from the pulpits of congregations with the message of getting away from the church's business and focusing on God's mission. The mission of God is simple. We are to love the Lord God with all our heart, our soul and our strength. But, Jesus takes this even further when He says that we are also to love one another as He has loved us. This is more difficult because we are also to love our enemies. None of the above is possible in our present state of sinfulness apart from the powerful work of the Holy Spirit.

We search eagerly for that special relationship with God that helps to define who we are or why we exist. The former is an individual assessment that will be better understood as this study begins to unfold. The latter is simple, but complex, depending on your relationship with the Lord Jesus Christ. We exist simply to love, worship, and serve God and Him alone. It becomes complicated because of our human sinful nature as well as our understanding of love. Again, as this study progresses, the individual will begin to understand and prayerfully realize what true "God Love" or unconditional love means. In addition to this, the Believer should understand why this is important to experiencing true spiritual power. In Acts 1:8, the Lord Jesus Christ demonstrated for Believers, at His ascension, that Spiritual Power is simply God's Power! With this power comes the authority to stand against the evil that is working hard to overcome those whom God loves. The glory of the living God can only be manifested through the empowering work of the Holy Spirit. The role of the Holy Spirit is primarily to comfort, equip, and strengthen the Believer on their journey to a full relationship with Jesus Christ.

The understanding of the role of the Holy Spirit in the life of the Believer should be viewed as a two-way street. Those who seek after that full relationship with Jesus Christ with all their hearts may also realize that the relationship requires some personal sacrifice as well as a receptive spirit. The Holy Spirit does not just force His way into a person's life and take over their spirit, that is possession. The Holy Spirit is given freely by God the Father to those who are willing to surrender their lives to a life with His Son Jesus Christ. The person must first be willing to receive the gift of the Holy Spirit before God can work in their lives. The common misconception in some denominations today is that one must first be able to speak in tongues or they are not saved. That cannot be farther from the truth. In fact, the Apostle Paul, in 1 Corinthians 14, gives a very pointed discussion pertaining to this topic. In this study, we will not deal specifically with the manifestations of the gifts of the Spirit. Rather, you will be introduced to the teachings of Jesus Christ found in His first sermon with the foundation in the beatitudes. Jesus gave us, in the Beatitudes, how to grow into that person after God's own heart, like King David and particularly like Jesus Himself.

God's Spiritual Power Manifested

> *When the Day of Pentecost had fully come, they were all with one accord in one place. And suddenly there came a sound from heaven, as of a rushing mighty wind, and it filled the whole house where they were sitting. Then there appeared to them divided tongues, as of fire, and one sat upon each of them. And they were all filled with the Holy Spirit and began to speak with other tongues, as the Spirit gave them utterance.* (Acts 2:1-4)

The understanding of the Spirit of God as seen in the first two chapters of Acts is in many ways four-fold. The notion of the Spirit and the evidence of that same Spirit was seen in scripture as a rushing wind, water, fire, and earth. The common misconception of the function or even the physical evidence, as seen in scripture, of the Spirit of God in relation to the faith of those who serve Him, is that God is God and very impersonal to His creation. This could not be further from the truth. Many elemental religions have given credit to the elements (namely wind, water, earth and fire) and the gods they understood to be their guiding force. God, as we as Christian understand Him, is creation as well as creator. Those religions believe that their salvation is found in the glory of nature.

We believe in God as our Father, Creator, and true and only God in three distinct persons (the Trinity). The Son, living and physical through Jesus Christ, is the personification of the Father. The Holy Spirit or Spirit of God is the person of the trinity that has the power and authority of the Father through the faith, focus, and love of the Son. Because of the death and resurrection of the Son from the physical human sacrifice, all of creation was affected to the point that even nature itself cried out to God for redemption.

SPIRIT POWER – A RUSHING AND VIOLENT WIND

> *And suddenly there came a sound from heaven, as of a rushing mighty wind, and it filled the whole house where they were sitting.*   (Acts 2:2)

A truly misunderstood concept when studying the Holy Spirit is the manifestations of the Spirit outside the physical body, but affecting the senses. The Spirit touches the Believer and has touched the Believer since God walked in the Garden with Adam and Eve. Jesus used the wind in an analogy when speaking with Nicodemus, a Pharisee and a member of the Sanhedrin. Jesus said,

> *"The wind blows where it wishes, and you hear the sound of it, but cannot tell where it comes from and where it goes. So is everyone who is born of the Spirit."*   (John 3:8)

This is, by any understanding, an obscure statement made by Jesus. But, the teachings of the Spirit of God are the hardest to understand because He is something we cannot see. You can see and feel His effects in the life of serving Christ. The overwhelming work of the Spirit of God in the Believer's life is seen and felt in the change that takes place. People observing from the outside can see the changes more so than the Believer themselves. The only restrictions placed on the Holy Spirit are rooted in the Believer. In Matthew 27 verse fifty, when Jesus gave up the spirit, verses fifty-one through fifty-three, all the elements cried out!

The Apostles were all gathered in the upper room, one hundred and twenty individuals. The sound as a violent wind roared through the room where they were crowded. The Spirit had blown and covered them all in one moment. The power of God manifested in the element of wind. The implications of this say that they were covered throughout with the power of God. Every part of their being was involved in this event.

SPIRIT POWER – THE SPIRIT IGNITES AND WARMS LIKE A FIRE FOR SERVICE

> *Therefore thus says the Lord God of hosts: "Because you speak this word, Behold, I will make My words in your mouth fire, And this people wood, And it shall devour them.* (Jeremiah 5:14)

> *Then I said, "I will not make mention of Him,*
> *Nor speak anymore in His name."*
> *But His word was in my heart like a burning fire*
> *Shut up in my bones; I was weary of holding it back,*
> *And I could not.* (Jeremiah 20:9)

Moses – God speaking with Moses through a burning bush on fire but not consumed (Exodus 3) – *Presence, Revelation*

Moses and Israelites – God leading His people out of Egypt by a pillar of smoke by day and pillar of fire by night (Exodus 13) – *Protection*

Elijah – God sends down fire and consumes the altar and offering of Elijah, even the water around altar. (1 Kings 18) *Power*

Elijah – Elijah taken up to heaven in a whirlwind with a chariot of fire pulled by horses of fire. (2 Kings 2:11) *Power, Revelation*

Isaiah – Isaiah is purified by the touch of a glowing coal from the altar of God to his lips as he was commissioned for service. (Isaiah 6) *Presence, Revelation, Power, Purification*

In the New Testament, the idea concerning fire seems to be associated with both redemption and judgment. John the Baptist told his disciples in Matthew 3:11 that "I indeed baptize you with water unto repentance, but He who is coming after me is mightier than I, whose sandals I am not worthy to carry. He will baptize you with the Holy Spirit and fire." God's power can be seen in all that He does in His people. The most vivid accounts of God's power are fire in Christ's Revelation to the Apostle John on the Island of Patmos. Both examples of judgment and redemption are seen in very explicit detail. The visions chronicled by John in the Book of Revelation have proven to be a work of confusion for some and intense fascination for many others. The visions given to John for God's people are intended to bring conviction and fear to God's people. Many avoid this section of scripture because they believe that it does not have anything to do with them. They glorify the first chapter and the last, but consider the middle twenty chapters to be too abstract and could not possibly be talking about them. This is farther from the truth!

The concept of fire in Revelation is very forth telling and speaks to the unveiling of the Truth most people want write off as fiction or hype. Consider the fact that Jesus was showing John the final interaction of God with his creation as a way of reconciliation. On the other side of the coin there can be seen a mighty spiritual war that is in constant flux, where the adversary, Satan, is at work to destroy any chance of reconciliation.

Understanding and believing the reality of this war and that human beings are in the middle of the turmoil, should bring the Believer to a new level of belief. But it does not. Instead, they decide that it is fantasy and a work of a creative mind, nothing more. When this happens, Satan wins because the church begins to settle for the things of this earth and give up on the glory and wealth of eternity in heaven. That is the great deception!

The concepts of judgment and redemption are found right at the core of the belief system of the true Believer. There is no gray area when it comes to God's work in and through His people. In terms of judgment, fire relates to eternal damnation. Also, as seen in revelation, hell or damnation is reserved for the devil and his angels. It was not created by God for His created humans. So, in consideration of the flip side of the coin, fire can also be seen in terms of redemption. The connection with redemption is less accepted by mainline Believers. When a Believer goes through the fire, it is difficult and goes against the grain of the prosperity movement and those who submit to the belief of "once saved always saved." These are among those doctrines that paint great walls of deception.

Scripture tells the Believer the Truth as relayed through the Son Jesus Christ by way of His Holy Spirit. For a Believer to grow into the fullness of the relationship with God the Father, a Believer will go through the fire because the fire refines and makes pure. This is what the Believer must do to be sanctified holy before a Holy God. When metal is placed in the fire, it is refined and impurities are removed so that it can become pure. It can then be formed into the instrument of service for which it was intended. So, it is with God. He allows His people to be thrown into the fire so that the impurities in their lives can be forged out and He can form them into the vessels to be used for His glory.

The Role of the Holy Spirit in the Acts of the Apostles

But you shall receive power when the Holy Spirit has come upon you; and you shall be witnesses to Me in Jerusalem, and in all Judea and Samaria, and to the end of the earth. (Acts1:8)

The part of this power that tends to turn most Christians away from desiring it concerns primarily with the notion of being "baptized with the Holy Spirit." Jesus states that for us in Acts 1:5, "… for John truly baptized with water, but you shall be baptized with the Holy Spirit not many days from now." This is a gift! When Christ ascended into heaven, He sent His Holy Spirit. This is the same Holy Spirit that was His power, authority, and guiding force while living among His people. This is the same Holy Spirit He sent for us so that we could truly experience the kingdom of God now, in our life. True Kingdom of God power or Spiritual Power will be experienced if you only let God be God. Allow the Holy Spirit to use you to the glory of God. The most popular example of this experience was evidenced by those present in the upper room on the day celebrated as the Day of Pentecost. Acts Chapter 2 gives the reader a vivid account and resulting scene of God's power when given to individuals who truly seek His power.

What is not normally understood here is that the Holy Spirit or the Spirit of God enabled these individuals to speak the native languages of all those who were present. The people present made the most telling statement:

> *And He said to them, "It is not for you to know times or seasons which the Father has put in His own authority. But you shall receive power when the Holy Spirit has come upon you; and you shall be witnesses to Me in Jerusalem, and in all Judea and Samaria, and to the end of the earth."* (Acts 1:7-8)

Why was this important? Why was it so important that God used this gift to reach all these people? Because, when a person was spoken to in their own native language, it became personal and you spoke to the heart of that individual. In the latter part of verse eleven it stated that

> *"Men of Galilee, why do you stand gazing up into heaven? This same Jesus, who was taken up from you into heaven, will so come in like manner as you saw Him go into heaven."*

During this time in history, the Roman Empire was on the rise and had a foothold on the people of Judah. Also, during the Jewish Festivals and feasts, such as Passover, the Roman rule become particularly harsh, as seen in the trial and death of Jesus Christ. A common language was used for specific acts of business. If you were dealing with the Romans or wanted to understand what they were saying to you, Latin was the language, especially on the political level. When selling in the markets throughout the empire, thanks to Alexander the Great and his accomplishments, Greek was the common language spoken. If you were to deal personally with a person in their home, their native tongue was more personal. In Judah, it would have been Aramaic and in the Temple pure Hebrew was the spoken tongue. The difference between proper speech and common speech is more idioms or slang phrases in the Aramaic. So, understanding why God chose to speak to them in their native, in home, tongues, shows that God, when He speaks, He speaks to the heart of the individual.

The resulting action of the people following Peter's extended speech was nothing short of incredible. Peter started by calling them all back to the scriptures when he cites Joel 3:1-5. He interprets this outpouring of the spirit as an introduction into the last days – but unlike Joel, who was speaking to the people of Judah, Peter spoke to all humanity. The entirety of the speech set the stage for the beginning of the formation of the church. In Acts 2, beginning in verse thirty-seven, was the response of the people to the calling of the Spirit:

> *Now when they heard this, they were cut to the heart, and said to Peter and the rest of the apostles, "Men and brethren, what shall we do?"*

> *Then Peter said to them, "Repent, and let every one of you be baptized in the name of Jesus Christ for the remission of sins; and you shall receive the gift of the Holy Spirit."* (Acts 2:37-38)

On that day, the Lord added to the number of disciples by three thousand souls. That is spiritual power! Now, did they just leave these people at the altar to seek and work out their own salvation with fear and trembling? NO! The next verse sums up what happens when the Spirit and not humanity leads souls into a spiritually powered relationship with Jesus Christ. They devoted themselves to the Apostles teachings, fellowship, to the breaking of bread and prayer. They became a community. More than a community, they became a family as children of the living God.

The last verse of Acts Chapter 2 is evidence that truth and power the spirit brings to those who enter a deeper relationship with Jesus Christ stretches far beyond any human understanding. "And they continued steadfastly in the apostles' doctrine and fellowship, in the breaking of bread, and in prayers." They would sell all their possessions and distribute to those who were in need. They were all together day after day. At home and in the Temple, they shared with one another through the spirit, a life that was far beyond any life otherwise imagined. Who would have thought that the sinner groveling and begging at the gate could truly have a new life of family coupled with spiritual power? Who would have imagined that a tax collector, adulteress, and some fishermen would step forward and change the world? But, through the power of the Spirit of God, we are more than conquerors. We are children of the Living God through His Son and the power of His Holy Spirit.

Many pastors and teachers teach *religion* or even Jesus without the mention of the Spirit. The role of the Holy Spirit is fundamental to understanding our relationship with Jesus Christ. Think of God the Father as being all around us, protecting us. Jesus Christ, His Son, as "God with us" or *Emmanuel* as teaching us. So, God the Holy Spirit, being within us, as guiding and leading us to a better life with Him. As this study begins to unfold, the understanding, acceptance, and fulfillment of a more spiritual life will become a part of the reality of real life. Remember, that God is Life, God is Power, and more than anything else, God is Love. It is through His never ceasing love that He sent His Son and because of His Son that the Holy Spirit was sent to bring us a more spiritually powered life.

THE HOLY SPIRIT IN THE TEACHINGS OF JESUS

> *If you love Me, keep My commandments. And I will pray the Father, and He will give you another Helper, that He may abide with you forever— the Spirit of truth, whom the world cannot receive, because it neither sees Him nor knows Him; but you know Him, for He dwells with you and will be in you.* (John 14:15-17)

The Spirit of God plays a large role in the teachings of Jesus, especially as expressed in the Gospel of John. The Holy Spirit was the key element in Jesus preparing the disciples for the ministries they were called out from the world to do for God. The disciples did not understand what he was talking about because they were not yet filled with the Spirit. As they traveled with Jesus daily and observed the wonders and signs, we must ask ourselves the question, "Why didn't they see or even feel the Spirit of God around them?" Well, maybe they did. Let us consider the fact that the Spirit of God, that was in Jesus the man, is what drew them to him when they were called. Consider also that it was God Himself who drew them into the relationship. The Word incarnate or God in the flesh dwelt among His creation. The disciples, as human beings, should have felt or at least sensed something beyond their own understanding while in the presence of Jesus.

The farewell discourses found in the Gospel of John Chapters 14 through 16 follow one of the most humbling passages toward the disciples from Jesus in the Gospel of John. The previous chapters, namely 12 and 13, started with Mary, sister of Lazarus, the one raised from the dead, and Martha, anointing the feet of Jesus with a pound of costly perfume and drying them with her hair in Chapter 12. The next chapter, 13, Jesus washed the disciples' feet following their last supper together. The betrayal of Judas Iscariot followed the washing of the feet. This is unique in the fact that Jesus washed the feet of the one who would betray him. The consideration to see here is that the disciples were witnesses to both and participants in the latter. Jesus teaches His last lesson to the disciples as He demonstrates the culmination of all that He has taught in one simple humiliating experience, "Love one another as I have loved you." Unconditionally love one another to the point of humbling yourself before one another. Washing a person's feet in the days of Jesus was left for the lowly servants of the household. For Jesus, their master, the master of the universe, to humble Himself that low as to wash His disciples' feet was a demonstration of unconditional love or in the Greek language "agape." The most telling part of this experience for the disciples was that Judas Iscariot, who would betray him, was one of those whose feet He washed and He washed them as He did the others. There was no indication that he was different or that he was going to do something to Jesus. Jesus treated him as He did all the others. This is Holy-Spirit-Godly-Love demonstrated in its purest form.

Jesus, in the final words to His disciples, begins to set the stage for His disciples in preparation for them to receive the same Spirit that He shared with the Father in heaven. He tried to direct their concerns from Him leaving to the comforting prospect of the one that He would send in His place. In Chapter 14, Jesus says to His disciples:

> *"I will not leave you orphans; I will come to you.*
>
> *A little while longer and the world will see Me no more, but you will see Me. Because I live, you will live also. At that day you will know that I am in My Father, and you in Me, and I in you. He who has My commandments and keeps them, it is he who loves Me. And he who loves Me will be loved by My Father, and I will love him and manifest Myself to him."* (John 14:18-21)

The only way to maintain continuity between the Father, Son, and the disciples is by the power of the Holy Spirit. God's Spirit is a uniting power that does not tear away as to destroy, but He is a healing and reviving Spirit. As we will see in subsequent chapters, the reviving Spirit of God will bring a person to their knees before they can truly understand the gravity of what God requires of us. The disciples didn't understand this concept fully at this point in their relationship with Jesus. In verses 25 and 26, Jesus explains Himself further to his disciples:

> *"These things I have spoken to you while being present with you. But the Helper, the Holy Spirit, whom the Father will send in My name, He will teach you all things, and bring to your remembrance all things that I said to you."* (John 14:25-26)

Jesus saw that they were going to falter in their beliefs, but He also knew their heart. They would act out of fear. Christians today act out of impulse therefore they react out of fear. We see that the early Apostles were human and not super human followers of

Christ. Just as Jesus came as a human and suffered the same infirmities as humans did, even death, so it is with our understanding of the Apostles. They were human and had human weaknesses and tendencies. There lies the fundamental difference between The Christ and a sinful wretched humanity. Jesus is God. He experienced temptation as everyone else, but he lived without sin.

The Holy Spirit's role in the life of Jesus was as a guide, teacher, leader, communicator with the Father, and comforter. So, we can see the significance and the importance for our need of the Holy Spirit in our lives. Because of the impulse exhibited by humans in given situations, the Holy Spirit is the guide, teacher, leader, communicator, the one who empowers and enables, and at times a conscience for our otherwise sinful nature. The more room the Holy Spirit is given to move in a person's life, the closer to God they grow.

THE HOLY SPIRIT AND THE FORMATION OF THE CHURCH

And they stoned Stephen as he was calling on God and saying, "Lord Jesus, receive my spirit." Then he knelt down and cried out with a loud voice, "Lord, do not charge them with this sin." And when he had said this, he fell asleep. (Acts 7:59-60)

The experience of the disciples at Pentecost served as the marker for the beginnings in the formation of the church. As the church was formed, one sure thing was evident. The Holy Spirit was at the heart of its foundation and development. Without the work of the Holy Spirit, they were just another bunch of street preachers and they probably would have gone back to their former ways of life. But, their numbers began to grow because they were looking to the Holy Spirit for their authority and power to be the people called by God to be holy.

In Chapter 6 of Acts, further evidence of the work of the Holy Spirit was shown through the Apostles. Their openness and understanding of the power that the Holy Spirit possessed gave to those who sought for it a fearless resolve. This evidence was observed among the ones who received the power from the Spirit. There were seven men chosen from among the disciples by the Apostles to serve the widows of the Hellenists (Greeks). Many complaints had raised against the Hebrews that they were neglecting the Greek widows and treating them unfairly. The qualifications for these seven individuals set the standard for power and authority in the church. First, they had to be *filled* or *full* (πλήρεις – Greek or play-reis; meaning *full, complete, sufficient*) of the Spirit and wisdom. Second, they had to be men of good standing among their peers. This speaks volumes to the focus and integrity of those who were chosen. The Apostles and their disciples never anticipated the effect the Holy Spirit was having on people within their own assembly. Many of these Believers may not have ever seen Jesus Christ, but they were filled with the Holy Spirit and lived as though they had walked and talked with Him along with the Apostles. They believed because of the realness and power of the Holy Spirit in their lives. They were not just waiting on tables of Greek widows; they were living the power-driven life of the Holy Spirit, because they were ministering to all people. They listened to what the Father told them to do, empowered by the Holy Spirit.

Those individuals selected were chosen to minister to *all* people. They served the widows, the task for which they were chosen. But, they did their task in the power of the Holy Spirit and without fear. Fear is the number one cause of individuals to turn away from their calling in life. Fear is Satan's tool, his sword so to speak, to battle against those who stand and fight in the Spirit, doing the will of God.

One individual selected from among his peers to serve was Stephen. Stephen stands out so prominently because he was the first recorded martyr following the death of Jesus Christ. Beginning in Chapter seven of Acts, following Stephen's arrest, he was brought before the Sanhedrin where the High Priest asked him, "Are these charges true?" To that, Stephen replied to them, empowered by the Holy Spirit, and stood with his head high as he spoke. Stephen recounted the history of the Jewish people as it related to salvation history and the death and resurrection of Jesus Christ. Periodically, during his defense of the gospel, he stood in protest toward the Jewish people in that they were responsible for the rejection of those who were called by God to deliver them. The very ones they raise up in praise for their service to God are the ones they rejected. The stoning and death of Stephen was to be the event that gave way to scattering the followers of Jesus. This began the establishment of the "church." God, through the work of the Holy Spirit, provided a way for Christianity to spread throughout the known world in a short time. So, it was the work of the Holy Spirit through the individuals who were scattered that was the driving force God used to set the world on fire for service and love for the Lord Jesus Christ.

As the study continues, it will take a move from historical to personal. The teachings of Jesus concerning the basics of our belief as taught from the beginning of His ministry. The Holy Spirit and the understanding of the Spirit in everyday life are important to realizing who we are in relation to a loving and personal God. The Holy Spirit serves as a teacher, guide, leader, and at many times our conscience. But, we need to realize that the Holy Spirit is also our humbler, mediator, and most of all comforter and friend. The Spirit of God is not bad or evil or just trying to take away our fun, but He is the third person of the triune God. The Holy Spirit is God. He is the same God's Spirit that made communication with God the Father possible for God the Son, Jesus Christ. What a privilege to carry everything to God in prayer. What a wonderful sentiment and how true it is that God hears the prayers of those who are faithful to Him through the power of His Holy Spirit.

WHERE DO WE GO FROM HERE?

The whole of this study is to bring the student of Scripture and the one who is eagerly seeking after a more intimate relationship with Jesus Christ into one in the power of the Holy Spirit.

The Holy Spirit as God's Spirit is misunderstood by many Christians today. As you seek the face of God and that relationship with Christ, seek the Spirit of God to fill your life and guide your path. Your life will never be the same! Do not seek the Spirit of God for the gifts of the Spirit, they will come with your faith,

> *For I say, through the grace given to me, to everyone who is among you, not to think of himself more highly than he ought to think, but to think soberly, as God has dealt to each one a measure of faith.*   (Romans 12:3)

Seek and rely on the Holy Spirit and you will do far more in Jesus' name than you will ever imagine. Your whole life, every area of your life, will be changed forever! Stay the Course!

CLOSING PRAYER:

Heavenly Father, through the sacrifice of Your Son Jesus Christ and in His name, I seek for Your cleansing Grace and Mercy to prepare me to be fully empowered for Your service with power of the Holy Spirit in my life. I give my life and heart to You whole and completely for Your service. In Jesus Name, Amen.

QUESTIONS FOR DISCUSSION

The Role of the Holy Spirit

1. How can the Holy Spirit be evidenced in the Believer's life and why is this important to a growing relationship with Jesus Christ?

2. We must first have a scriptural understanding of God's Spirit. In Scripture, what are ways the Holy Spirit has manifested? Why?

3. Why are the four elements important in understanding the Spirit and the power of God and authority given?

4. When those in the upper room received the Holy Spirit, that was the "eureka" moment for them? How did it effect their understanding of Jesus, God, and the world?

5. The Holy Spirit played a critical role in Jesus' teachings. How much more powerful would our testimony, preceding, and teaching be if we would allow the Holy Spirit to take the authority?

6. When the church was scattered after the martyrdom of Stephen, why do you think the Christian movement exploded on the world scene instead dying out? How does that make you new in Christianity today?

2

Living Our Relationship to God

Humility

Let nothing be done through selfish ambition or conceit, but in lowliness of mind let each esteem others better than himself. Let each of you look out not only for his own interests, but also for the interests of others.

Let this mind be in you which was also in Christ Jesus.
(Philippians 2:3-5)

Understanding the idea of humility, we must first listen to the teachings of Jesus concerning this topic. If there was any one person who could teach on the life of humility, it is the person of the Lord Jesus Christ. Humility is the starting point from which a person must begin on a journey that is full of hills, valleys, and mountains. At times, it doesn't seem fair or it doesn't appear that we can make it through the next moment. But, Jesus introduced to the disciples the way to be focused on the Lord and Him alone and not let the trials of the world interfere with the relationship being established with God. The Holy Spirit plays an intricate role in this process, because it cannot be accomplished through our own power. It is only through the guiding power of the Holy Spirit that we can achieve true personal spiritual formation.

Jesus began His ministry by teaching principles that were basic characteristics of individuals who are set apart by God to be holy. In the Beatitudes, Matthew 5:3-12, he outlines the path for us to pursue. Each step on that path consists of trials. A death to self that is such a prominent part of the battle between the will of the spirit and the sinful nature of the individual is found at its core.

The next chapters of this study will bring the reader to the point of considering their own sinful nature. Even more important, they will understand how the Spirit of God can work with them, to empower them, to achieve a spiritually formed life. As you look deeper into your own understanding of yourself, keep in mind the sacrifice made on Calvary's Cross by our Lord and Savior Jesus Christ. The Apostle Paul tells us in his letter to the Roman church that:

> *I beseech you therefore, brethren, by the mercies of God, that*
> *you present your bodies a living sacrifice, holy, acceptable to God,*
> *which is your reasonable service.*   (Romans 12:1)

God's mercy towards us was demonstrated on that cross embodied in His Son Jesus Christ. So, when you think that this study is probing too harshly or digging too deep or getting too personal, remember the living sacrifice that was given so that you would have eternal life.

HUMILITY: STRENGTH FOR SALVATION

Blessed are the poor in spirit,
For theirs is the kingdom of heaven. (Matthew 5:3)

Humility, as defined by the world, is associated with weakness. As Jesus states to his disciples, in the first beatitude, that a person must be poor in spirit to inherit the kingdom of heaven. He says this with the understanding that He is speaking to fallen humanity and with that comes a sinful nature. So, what is meant by poor in spirit? Who can measure up to the standard that is set by this statement? At the most basic of Christian attributes lays Humility. No,

Humility is not a weakness, but strength. Being "poor in spirit," means to be humbled or to be poor in your own spirit to give way to God's Spirit. When we try to do God's will in our own strength, we fail. When we think that we have all the answers and that no one else is right, we have separated ourselves from a possible better way. The greatest individual example of humility found in scripture was in the life and death of Jesus. Paul's letter to the Philippian church gives us an understanding of the perfect example set for us by Christ Himself.

> *Let this mind be in you which was also in Christ Jesus, who, being in the form of God, did not consider it robbery to be equal with God, but made Himself of no reputation, taking the form of a bondservant, and coming in the likeness of men. And being found in appearance as a man, He humbled Himself and became obedient to the point of death, even the death of the cross.*
> (Philippians 2:5-8)

He was and is God in the flesh. The Gospel of John chapter 1 verse fourteen states that "The Word became flesh and dwelt among us." Our understanding of humility cannot fathom the depths of Love that God has for His creation. He made Himself as His creation to connect with them on their level. When communicating with a small child, you lower yourself normally to their level, physically, so you can communicate with them eye to eye. God lowered Himself down to our lowest level and demonstrated true obedience and humility for us to love and connect with Him. In humility, it is seen in scripture that our first step to understanding a true relationship with Jesus Christ and God the Father is through a poor spirit of our own.

Jesus was obedient unto death, even the death on the cross. Crucifixion was the most humiliating, painful, and torturous forms of execution known. Jesus said in his prayer to the Father in the Garden of Gethsemane prior to his arrest, *not my will but Your Will be done.* He humbled himself before God the Father and separated his human spirit from the Spirit of God. The Holy Spirit is the way we receive our power. In human nature, humility is not a common practice, but for a person to enter the presence of God, they must first and foremost humble themselves.

The prophet Isaiah experienced true humility when he stood before the throne of God at his commissioning. He saw God on the throne of heaven with seraphim and cherubim and all the heavenly hosts present. The robe of God filled the temple and Isaiah realized his insignificance in comparison to the heavenly hosts. Isaiah said:

> *"Woe is me, for I am undone!*
> *Because I am a man of unclean lips,*
> *And I dwell in the midst of a people of unclean lips;*
> *For my eyes have seen the King,*
> *The Lord of hosts."*   (Isaiah 6:5)

Isaiah humbled himself and cried out to the Lord through his unworthiness. The one thing that an individual tends to forget is that God is faithful and just. He does not want His people to seek Him for the purpose to solely benefit them, but to seek after Him with a humbled heart. Isaiah experienced spiritual power at his commissioning and throughout his ministry with the Lord. The power came not by his personal accomplishments, but in the giving of himself in humility to the Lord. This power was given for the salvation of the nation of Judah and all of Israel.

Humility: Paul's Prospective in Terms of The Church

> *I, therefore, the prisoner of the Lord, beseech you to walk worthy of the calling with which you were called, with all lowliness and gentleness, with longsuffering, bearing with one another in love, endeavoring to keep the unity of the Spirit in the bond of peace.*   (Ephesians 4:1-3)

Paul understood the concept of humility more than any one human could possibly know, except for Jesus Christ Himself. He was humbled on the road to Damascus as a witness to the risen Lord. Preceding this event, he was the most feared man to stand against the Christians. The Pharisee Saul (later known as Paul) had to humble himself as he stood before the risen Christ and give account for his actions against Him. Every known form of persecution was performed on Paul, but despite all the pain and anguish he continued and persevered with a humbled heart before God. He understood the importance of humbling himself before God. We are creatures of an eternal God that created everything, the universe, including humanity. We should not believe ourselves to be holy and in control of things more than God, because He does not have to show us mercy. We deserve justice and justice for us is eternal damnation. Paul understood this and he lived his life with this fear of God in mind.

When you consider that the church is made up of people, people by their very nature who are sinful and have sinful tendencies; the natural order suggests that strife and chaos should result, and does. But, Paul gives us another suggestion. He suggests that, despite the diversity of natures and personalities, God uses diversity to form unity within the body. This is understood by the individuals being "… completely humble and gentle." The other part of that is similar in its intent saying; "be patient, bearing with one another in love." The idea of unity here finds its foundation in humility and God's unconditional love. It is one of the hardest things to do, but we are commanded to do it, by the Lord Jesus Christ. When a person truly humbles themselves before God and humanity, there are unlimited eternal ways to be used for His glory. Humility means doing nothing for your own benefit but for the glory of God alone.

There are three passages that are frequently referred to when discussing the notion of spiritual gifts: They are Romans 12, 1 Corinthians 12, and Ephesians 4. In these letters to struggling churches, struggling much like we are today, Paul sets the stage for discussing the concept of spiritual gifts on the foundation of unity and love. Within each of these portions of scripture, he places as the one key element to experiencing true unity and Christ love is humility. In the Christian faith, humility is not a weakness but a prerequisite to living a life of holy commitment to Christ. In all three of these passages, there needs to be noted a commonality found in the order by which details are to be considered.

In his letter to the Romans, Paul opens the twelfth chapter with a call to humility. We are called to offer our bodies as living sacrifices. A living sacrifice you must give up something. But this living sacrifice must be holy and pleasing to God. As we have seen in Isaiah chapter six, Isaiah saw the wretchedness of his own soul. This cannot be seen apart from a truly humbled heart. Paul sets this idea to a higher standard when he uses the term transformed. A prideful individual cannot be transformed. The only way to be transformed is to turn the pride into humility. He says:

> *And do not be conformed to this world, but be transformed by the renewing of your mind, that you may prove what is that good and acceptable and perfect will of God.* (Romans 12:2)

How will you possibly be able to know the will of God? Paul plainly states that it is through the transformation of your mind and that can only be accomplished through a humbled heart. In the next verse, he made a pointed statement referring to the natural outflow from a mind that is transformed. He said,

> *For I say, through the grace given to me, to everyone who is among you, not to think of himself more highly than he ought to think, but to think soberly, as God has dealt to each one a measure of faith.* (Romans 12:3)

God gives us the strength to fall on our knees and become humble, obedient servants of the living God. We are to humble ourselves as living sacrifices to know God's good, pleasing and perfect Will, not only for our lives but also for His eternal plan. Christians should disregard the notion that God's Will is only for this world; because what we do contributes to the "Big Picture" of eternity for God's pleasure. Remember, Paul speaks of being a humbled living sacrifice. This is setting the stage for the understanding of the proper knowledge of spiritual gifts.

The next letter Paul wrote to a church concerning spiritual gifts is to the church in Corinth. The church in Corinth was very gifted spiritually, but they were divided. Pride filtered into the assembly of Believers and they began to separate into groups as were focused on their gifts. Each one thought that their gift was more important than the others. The most problem came with the misuse of the gift of tongues. There were groups within the church at Corinth that believed you must have the gift of tongues. There are those today, entire denominations, which believe this as true. Pride was at the heart of the problems in Corinth. The pride that says "I am better than you because I speak in tongues!" or "You are not saved if you don't speak in tongues!" This is a lie spun from Satan himself! At the cornerstone of Paul's teaching to the Corinthian church was love. Not just any love, but God's unconditional, sacrificial love (Greek – αγαπέ or agape'). For the church at Corinth to experience true spiritual formation and power, they should see the "most excellent way" in love and humility.

At the beginning of Chapter 13, Paul said:

> *Though I speak with the tongues of men and of angels, but have not love, I have become sounding brass or a clanging cymbal. And though I have the gift of prophecy, and understand all mysteries and all knowledge, and though I have all faith, so that I could remove mountains, but have not love, I am nothing. And though I bestow all my goods to feed the poor, and though I give my body to be burned, but have not love, it profits me nothing.*
> (1 Corinthians 13:1-3)

The love that is the basis for the unity through the Holy Spirit and the use of spiritual gifts per the commands of God is rooted in humility. For an individual to experience any real work of the Holy Spirit, as was experienced in the upper room with the disciples of Jesus, they need to be rooted in humility and the true love of God. Love of God dictates a denial of oneself. Paul continues as he lists the characteristics true love that follows the will of God:

Love suffers long and is kind; love does not envy; love does not parade itself, is not puffed up, does not behave rudely, does not seek its own, is not provoked, thinks no evil; does not rejoice in iniquity, but rejoices in the truth; 7 bears all things, believes all things, hopes all things, endures all things. (1Corinthians 13:4-7)

When we love as God wants us to love, there must be acts of selfless humility that not only draws the attention on something else but also draws the attention away from the person doing the act. Random acts of kindness or servant evangelism has become a phenomenon in the whole notion of evangelism and its direction in the church. There must be an understanding that unconditional sacrificial love is at the root of anything that we choose to do in the service of the Lord. It should not be done with an expectation of reward in this life or the next. Even if a person does random acts of kindness, they should do it with total humility and focus on God and Him alone. As we can see in the "love" passage above, all the characteristics of love have as an underlining pretense of humility. Without it, one cannot achieve the level of love Paul is trying to accomplish. If you look closely to each example, they tend to be characteristics of humility. There are numerous further writings of Paul that point to the idea of humility, but they will come up later in the study.

HUMILITY IN THE TEACHINGS OF JESUS

Humility is, at its basic understanding, one of the most important things a human being can accomplish. Its flipside is Pride. Pride is a foundational sin. At the base understanding of the fall of humanity and even the fall of Lucifer from heaven, *pride* is the cornerstone. Jesus began His ministry with this statement in His first sermon; *"Blessed are the poor in spirit, for theirs is the kingdom of Heaven."*

The sinful nature that humanity has at its base is the primal sin of pride. So it is hard, and a definite struggle, for someone to humble themselves, truly bow in humility, before God. It is unnatural.

Yes, God did create humanity in His own image, but along with that came Free Will. We are given a choice. There are choices being made moment by moment everyday by individuals, some good and some bad. Humility is a choice. Jesus started His first sermon, the Sermon on the Mount or The Sermon on the Plain, with His first words telling His disciples to humble themselves.

The Beatitudes are well known within the church and its teachings, but are not truly understood in their individual elements. When they are taken collectively, there is no question that they are to be known as the standard of living the Christian life. But there is another consideration to be open to when viewing the Beatitudes and their teachings. Look at each and consider them as stepping stones to a process of spiritual growth. The first or initial step in the whole process is to be "poor in spirit." Poor in spirit is to be poor in one's own spirit or a sense of unworthiness. In other words, unworthiness is humility at its most basic point. Why did Jesus begin His ministry by making this statement? Why did He see the need to set a standard that would go against the grain of human nature? Well, let's consider for a moment human nature. Humans by nature are sinful as well as selfish. Should we, for a moment, think that God should lower His expectations of His creation, just because we are not like God? God knows the capability of His people. Not everybody is at the same level spiritually, but the ability to be open to the work of the Spirit of God in one's life is available to all people. They only must be open to the Spirit.

Looking back to the original dedication of the Temple that was built by Solomon for the Lord, God gives a clear command with a pointed condition that still resonates even today. He said to the people of Israel;

> *If My people who are called by My name will humble themselves, and pray and seek My face, and turn from their wicked ways, then I will hear from heaven, and will forgive their sin and heal their land.* (2 Chronicles 7:14)

God gives a simple command, but it has a hard condition. They had four basic conditions that they were to do to remain in a right relationship with God. The first was to *humble themselves.* The second condition was to *pray.* The third condition was to *seek His face.* The fourth, crucial to certain change in one's life, *turn from their wicked ways.* We are no different than the people of Israel. We have the same God who has also called us, and all who serve Christ after us, to follow Him. How can we think that we are any better than they were in their relationship with God? God chose countless people, from the creation of the universe to the present, to accomplish His eternal purpose. The condition of the heart of the individual is the common denominator. Noah, in faith and humility toward God, built a ship to God's specification in a time when rain was rare. Abram, who followed the call of God in faith and humility when nobody else understood, set out for a land promised by God to establish a nation of people that will be set well after his time. Moses, who humbled himself before God, was called to lead the nation of Israel out of the land of Egypt after four hundred years of oppression. Each of these individuals were called out because of their humility before a mighty God. So, it was with Solomon and the dedication of the Temple of God. If the people would set out to do the things God asked of them, **THEN** He will hear from heaven and forgive them of their sins and heal their land. He asked four things and in return He gave them three things.

Humility in the whole scheme of God's plan is at the core of our foundational understanding of God and our relationship with Him. When Jesus said, *"Blessed are the poor in spirit, for theirs is the kingdom of heaven,"* He saw full well the big picture and the impact this statement would have on those who chose to follow Him. When we begin to humble ourselves, and see God for who He is, then we will be able to love Him in spirit and in truth. It is not in the nature of humanity to take the difficult path. The common conception of the sinful nature is to follow the path of least resistance. The path of the cross and humility is not a wide one, but one that is narrow with many pot holes and ditches on either side. The reward at the end this journey, if we chose to follow it, is life eternally with the risen Christ. We must learn from Christ's teachings and especially from His example. This is not a new idea. God has been demonstrating His love for all creation from the beginning, but we just rationalize our way out of the relationship. All He asks for us to do is to start humbling ourselves before Him and seek His face and turn back to Him in humility as living sacrifices. He will, in turn, be our God and love us unconditionally with a love that is unfathomable to any human understanding.

WHERE DO WE GO FROM HERE?

Humility, in its purest form, is found in the total abandonment of oneself and the realization that you are lost. The Holy Spirit is the guiding light that shines before us and leads us out of the darkness of sin.

You must first humble yourself before God and surrender your heart and life completely to Jesus Christ. Recognizing your need for Jesus gives you the ability and availability to receive the power from on high with the Holy Spirit. Humbling oneself is the key to being able to grow in the Spirit. God gives grace to the humble.

Likewise, you younger people, submit yourselves to your elders.
Yes, all of you be submissive to one another,
and be clothed with humility, for
"God resists the proud,
But gives grace to the humble."

Therefore, humble yourselves under the mighty hand of God,
that He may exalt you in due time, casting all your care upon Him,
for He cares for you. (1 Peter 5:5-7)

Remember that a humble person is not a weak person, but is one who becomes among the strongest. If we are a person humble before the Lord, we are completely willing to receive everything that Holy Spirit has prepared for them. Why? Because they have

emptied themselves and are ready and willing to receive the power
from on high promised by Jesus for His service.

Closing Prayer:

*Most Gracious Heavenly Father, given all grace and glory to
You, I pray that You give me a clean heart and a humble spirit that I
may be the servant that you have called me out of the darkness to be,
In Jesus Name, Amen*

Questions for Discussion

Humility Before God

1.   How would you define a humble person?

2.   What is meant by "poor in spirit"? How do you define it in
     a Christian?

3.   Why would you view humility as the basis or foundation for
     the Christian faith?

3

THE NEED FOR RECONCILIATION TO GOD

PENITENCE

"Now, therefore," says the LORD,
"Turn to Me with all your heart,
With fasting, with weeping, and with mourning.
So rend your heart, and not your garments;
Return to the LORD your God,
For He is gracious and merciful,
Slow to anger, and of great kindness;
And He relents from doing harm."   (Joel 2:12-13)

As children of the living God, we need to understand that just because we are forgiven, that does not give us the free license to sin. We are not immune to sin. Yes! Chances are that we will need to repent about something that we have done or said or thought many times in the run of a day. As in the passage from the prophet Joel, we should repent and return to God.

What does it mean to repent? Repent means to change your mind or completely turn around in your thinking. Humility was the defining element that gave the Believer purpose and direction. Without humility, there is no repentance. Insight given into that relationship they were seeking, guided the individual to the point surrender and repentance. Repentance, on the other hand, is step two. The process spoken of by Jesus in the Beatitudes is the process by which a person grows closer and closer to God. Our understanding of the idea of repentance seems to be somewhat limited to the point of our salvation. The whole concept of repentance should be understood in terms of a daily opening of oneself to God and every moment seeking His forgiveness. As sinful creatures, we are not perfect and we can never be perfect as the world defines the perfection. God's concept of perfection is in terms of our relationship with Him. The more sin into the life of the Believer, the further away a person seems to get from God, and the more there seems to be a need for repentance. In the passage from Joel, there is seen God's eagerness to reconcile a relationship with His creation. But the terminology brings a sense of urgency in God's request. He tells us to *"Rend your hearts and not your garments."* He doesn't ask us to open our hearts to Him, but to "rend." The word *rend* means to *tear* your heart open.

The common tradition for the Jewish people as an act of repentance was to rend or tear their clothing. God specifically said to His people to rend their hearts and **NOT** their garments. Repentance, in other words, has a more urgent and visible meaning to the Jewish people. When Job lost all he possessed, including wealth, health and family, *Then Job arose, tore his robe, and shaved his head; and he fell to the ground and worshiped.* (Job 1:20) His actions speak louder than his words. Despite all that had happened to Job and his family, he still believed that he needed to fall into a posture of humble repentance before a mighty God. There was no question in Job's mind what to do, whether he was guilty of a sin or not. He was at the level of his relationship with God to know that God was just. The common act of the sinful nature is to rationalize on one end of the spectrum and to deny or even pass the blame in another direction. God told His people to rend or tear their hearts. They needed to truly be conscious of their repentance. He does not want those who are called by His name to love Him solely out of obligation, but to love Him with an open and transparent heart.

"Blessed are those who mourn, For they shall be comforted."
(Matthew 5:4)

For many years, the impression was given to the everyday reader of Scripture that this statement from the Beatitudes referred to mourning of the dead. This is an understandable misconception of that statement. When a person chooses to follow Christ, and surrenders their soul to Him, it is a commitment to a death to oneself. The literal meaning from the Greek language referring to *mourn* is the word όι πενθουντεζ or "those who grieve as for the dead." When Jesus is speaking to His disciples here, He had just chosen these disciples and began to teach them each step to take in the growth process to a closer relationship with God. The significance of this word is that it speaks to a death of self. Once a person, a true Believer, is humbled before God, then they must tear or rend the whole of their heart and soul open for God to cleanse them.

Paul tells us in his second letter to the Corinthian church that;

> *Therefore, if anyone is in Christ, he is a new creation; old things have passed away; behold, all things have become new. Now all things are of God, who has reconciled us to Himself through Jesus Christ, and has given us the ministry of reconciliation.*
> (2 Corinthians 5:17-18)

We are reconciled to Him because the old self has died with Christ and our new self has been raised from the dead. So, as Jesus made the statement "blessed are those who mourn," He saw that as a death of the old self or sinful nature. The person then will be comforted through the resurrecting power of the Holy Spirit in that the new self has been raised with Christ.

PROMISES TO TRUE REPENTANCE

The concept of repentance from sin seems to bring, to the one renouncing sin, a sense of loss in one's life. Many are afraid to release their sins because they do not understand what is to come. The belief for those turning from a life of sin to a life with Christ is that there are lists of "do's" and "don'ts" that are controlling factors to life. They no longer have control in their lives because they have given in to God. This misconception makes most people very hesitant to surrender to Christ and begin a relationship with Him.

The first step, humility, is defined by an extreme situation or event in one's life that makes them realize of their need for God. The second step, penitence or repentance, brings with it a sense of moral obligation to turn your life and walk away from sin. So, as we look at repentance, it must be realized that it does not mean that you give up having fun. Fun, as defined by the world, is tied to the sins of the world. Sins of the flesh are seen by the giving of yourself over to the pleasures of the body and the mind. But, the true follower of Christ knows that the life of a Christian is one of adventure, excitement, and more fun than can be imagined. Looking at this idea in the eyes of the usual hard driven life, there are five basic gifts that God gives to those who love Him with all their heart: Answer to Prayer, Pardon for Sin, Life Eternal, Comfort, and the Holy Spirit. These five, through the act of repentance, are the acts that drive the Christian toward a life of Spiritual Power.

PROMISES TO THOSE WITH A MOURNFUL SPIRIT:

1. Answer to Prayer

... if My people who are called by My name will humble themselves, and pray and seek My face, and turn from their wicked ways, then I will hear from heaven, and will forgive their sin and heal their land. (2 Chronicles 7:14)

When a person repents, they turn away from their sin and wickedness. The Lord God gives us four simple points to follow. First, He tells us to *humble* ourselves. Second, He tells us to simply *pray* or communicate with Him. This point brings us to repentance. To repent, a person must pray and open communication with God. Third, He tells us to *seek* His face. This is a continual process that the Christian will work to achieve for the remainder of their life. And fourth, the Christian must *turn* from their wicked ways. Repentance, as was noted earlier, means to turn into the opposite direction or to change one's mind. In other words, to completely turn away from sin and go to God. God answers prayer, but the Believer must truly turn their life around to His glory and not their own. The common misconception concerning repentance is that it is a one-shot deal at conversion. This couldn't be farther from the truth. Repentance is an everyday occurrence, if you are truly honest with yourself and God. No one is perfect except Christ alone. The moment you feel that you know it all is the moment that you have stepped away from God. Repentance is realizing your true unworthiness in your heart and soul. The one who is truly repentant continually and honestly before God will have their prayers answered.

2. Pardon for Sin

> *Let the wicked forsake his way,*
> *And the unrighteous man his thoughts;*
> *Let him return to the LORD,*
> *And He will have mercy on him;*
> *And to our God,*
> *For He will abundantly pardon.*   (Isaiah 55:7)

The second promise given by God to His repentant people is that He will pardon their sins. The condition that lies here is that they must turn from their previously wicked ways and turn to Him. In Isaiah 55, he tells us to forsake our wicked ways and turn from evil thoughts. Being truly repentant, a person must truly turn away completely from their bad lifestyles. But, more than this, the truly repentant person must cleanse their thoughts. The Lord God is not superficial but knows your thoughts as well as the condition of the heart. Despite this realization of the unworthiness of the human condition, God still wants to pardon sins. The condition and state of the human heart as standing before a Holy God is devastating. What humanity deserves in this light is to be destroyed, but God defends us through the everlasting love of His Son Jesus Christ and His ultimate sacrifice. The understanding of the term pardon can be seen considering the idea of a prison sentence. The difference between being on probation and being pardoned from a sentence for a crime is that when you are on probation you are monitored and restrictions are set on you until you have proven yourself ready. When a person is pardoned for a crime, you have been declared truly free to live life, apart from the restrictions. So, it is with the Christian who has truly repented from their sin. Jesus Christ gave His life in order that you would be pardoned for your sin and all the rights as heirs of heaven are given back to you. All He asks is that you love Him with all your heart, mind, soul and strength.

3. Life Eternal

> *For God so loved the world that He gave His only begotten Son, that whoever believes in Him should not perish but have everlasting life.*   (John 3:16)

> *But if a wicked man turns from all his sins which he has committed, keeps all My statutes, and does what is lawful and right, he shall surely live; he shall not die.*   (Ezekiel 18:21)

The Christian is promised life and life abundantly. The life of the repentant person is not an easy path. In fact, it is a life of many trials, but the rewards for enduring the trials far outweigh the painful and many times agonizing situations and events that begin to steer them down the road to righteousness. Life is a gift, not something you buy, trade, or sale on the open market.

During the time of the Protestant Reformation in the early fifteen-hundreds, the understanding of God was that of a Judge who sat on a throne ready to strike down the sinner. The light finally came on in the heart of Martin Luther when he realized that God did not want humanity to be destroyed but He wanted to give them life. God is a God of love and mercy and forgiveness, not of revenge and destruction who would rather condemn humanity to hell than to love them. The most famous verse in scripture is found in the Gospel of John at the end of Jesus' discussion with Nicodemus, a

Pharisee and a member of the Sanhedrin. The statement, in John 3:16, of the love of God is a testimony to God's endearing love for His people. In this verse, the only condition to eternal life is that a person, any person, believes in His Son and His sacrifice. He gave the life of His Son so that all humanity can have an opportunity for eternal life. In Ezekiel's verse, God gives three basic conditions to life. First the person turns away from all sin. The second condition is that they keep His decrees or commands. And third, do what is right in the eyes of the Lord God. For a person to meet the conditions of either verse, one must go back to the original basic premise that a person must turn completely away from sin and back to God. To believe something, you must first have a total transformation of the heart and become fully committed to it. Therefore, with this transformation comes true repentance.

4. Comfort

> *Blessed are those who mourn,*
> *For they shall be comforted.* (Matthew 5:4)

> *I say to you that likewise there will be more joy in heaven over*
> *one sinner who repents than over ninety-nine just persons who*
> *need no repentance.* (Luke 15:7)

The comfort found in our repentance is rooted in the hope to come; focused on eternity. When Jesus is teaching his disciples, concerning the idea of repentance, the notion of a deep sense of loss is felt. The person has lived a life and is asked to leave it behind and not look back. The newly penitent person has made a conscious decision to turn in the opposite direction and renounce their previous way of living. For many, it is a great loss. They have lived many years doing the same things and doing them the same ways. Now, they are told that they were wrong and immoral. This for some is devastating. It is like a death close to them. But, at the same time, it is very exciting and powerful because this is the work of the Holy Spirit. The Holy Spirit is the catalyst through which comfort and peace come to the individual. There is real comfort in the power of the Holy Spirit as He can work in a person's life. Comfort becomes one hope that is achieved through the work of God's grace. The beauty of it all is in Jesus' words in Luke 15:7. He says that there is more rejoicing in heaven when one person repents than for ninety-nine who do not need to repent. This is a very telling statement that He makes. In the same way, the Lord God or the good shepherd will leave the ninety-nine to go after the one lost. That is what gives comfort to those who mourn. We are not only forgiven but we are sought after without ceasing because of the agape unconditional love that God the Father through His Son Jesus Christ has for His people.

5. The Gift of the Holy Spirit

> *Then Peter said to them, "Repent, and let every one of you be baptized in the name of Jesus Christ for the remission of sins; and you shall receive the gift of the Holy Spirit."*   (Acts 2:38)

The real basis of true repentance is found in the resulting power that follows. There is great spiritual power at the point of repentance but this power needs to grow and be nurtured. This is the role of the Holy Spirit in the life of the individual. Upon the act of repentance, the Holy Spirit is given to the Christian for comfort, guidance and strength. More times than not, new Believers have a tendency of trying take the world by storm for Christ. As noble and pure hearted the intentions may be, the person must follow the lead of the Holy Spirit. As a guide, the Holy Spirit prepares the way for the Believer to minister. Also, as a guide, the Holy Spirit equips the Believer with what they need to minister. If a person climbs a mountain, they usually use a guide. Particularly, they will use a guide if they are unfamiliar with the mountain they are attempting to climb. This is how it is with the Holy Spirit. We are climbing mountains every day of our lives. Without the Holy Spirit to equip us for the journey and show us the way, we will surely stray from the path and fall into a ditch, a ravine or even off the mountain.

In terms of strength, the Holy Spirit gives us power and strength. The promise given by Jesus to His disciples at His ascension in Acts chapter one verse eight is testimony to the fact that it is a power from God. He said, "but you shall receive power when the Holy Spirit has come upon you; and you shall be witnesses to Me in Jerusalem, and in all Judea and Samaria, and to the end of the earth." This is the testimony of true pure power and strength. When you receive this power from God the Father, you will have power – God Power. Beyond that, you will be able to stand against the evil one and even your enemies. The apostle Paul states in his letter to the Romans Chapter 8 beginning in verse 31 that;

> *What then shall we say to these things? If God is for us, who can be against us? He who did not spare His Own Son, but delivered Him up for us all, how shall He not with Him also freely give us all things?* (Romans 8:31-32)

He goes on to say that;

> *Yet in all these things we are more than conquerors through Him who loved us. For I am persuaded that neither death nor life, nor angels nor principalities nor powers, nor things present nor things to come, nor height nor depth, nor any other created thing, shall be able to separate us from the love of God which is in Christ Jesus our Lord.* (Romans 8:37-39)

This can only be achieved through the sacrificial act of Jesus Christ and the Believer to allow the Holy Spirit to enter an unconditional relationship with them through agape or unconditional love. Just as Humans set conditions or even perimeters in their worldly lives, so they do with the Christian life. There is no box you can create that is big enough to keep God boxed up. The gift of the Holy Spirit is a gift. You receive a gift from the giver. Many Christians are afraid of the Holy Spirit because they do not understand. Jesus said in Acts chapter one that you *will* receive power *when* the Holy Spirit comes.

The Holy Spirit is a gift from God to be used. Jesus used the power of the Holy Spirit and He healed thousands and even raised many from the dead. The argument is "well, Jesus is Jesus, the Son of God! Of course, He can do all these things!" This is true, but what about Peter? He was empowered by the Holy Spirit to even raise Tabitha, known as Dorcas, from the dead in chapter nine of the book of Acts. In Chapter 20 of the Acts of the Apostles, Paul raised Eutychus from the dead following his fall from a third story window when he fell asleep and then fell to his death. We are promised the gift of the Holy Spirit. This is needed to do God's work the way He wants us to do it. He knows what is best for our lives and maybe it is time for the Christian to start realizing that God is in charge.

It is through the sacrificial acts of Jesus Christ that the Believer can stand with spiritual confidence and power before the enemies of God. More important, one will be able to stand before God the Father Himself. Repentance or a mournful spirit before God is at the foundation of where this life changing experience begins.

WHERE DO WE GO FROM HERE?

The penitent heart is one that recognizes the darkness and sin in their life and their need for a savior. The human being, as our nature, needs to maintain control in their life. The main faction in whether the individual is willing repent and completely yield to the work of the Holy Spirit in their life or not is if they are willing give control over to Jesus Christ.

It is true. You are not saved unless you repent and give life to Jesus Christ as your savior. It is one thing to acknowledge your sin and turn away from that sin. But, it is a completely more crucial way to turn and surrender control of one's whole life and heart. In doing this, you allow the Holy Spirit to perform the mighty work He was given to you accomplish.

Jesus answered, "Most assuredly, I say to you, unless one is born of water and the Spirit, he cannot enter the kingdom of God. (John 3:5)

The heart of repentance is one that knows that the void and need in their life is found Christ and Him alone. The Holy Spirit is the one who strengthens and guides the humble and repentant heart toward the saving mercy and grace of Christ in their life. Are you, as a person seeking after something more in your life, be willing to surrender full control of your life to equipping power of the Holy Spirit? He will set you free and your life will never be the same.

CLOSING PRAYER:

O, most gracious and merciful Father, take my life and heart for your glory. May you be glorified by my surrendered heart and life. Create in me a clean heart so that all that is within me can fully praise Your Holy Name! In Jesus Name, Amen.

DISCUSSION QUESTIONS

Penitent Before God

1. Which 5 basic gifts does God give to those who love him? Why is that important in the everyday Christian life?

2. How does your desperate need for repentance set you on the path of reconciliation with God?

3. Why is repentance an ongoing practice for Christians?

4. How does your need for reconciliation with God through repentance make you focus more on your relationships with one another?

4

The Power of Kindness

MEEKNESS

Blessed are the meek,
For they shall inherit the earth. (Matthew 5:5)

The idea of meekness, by many circles, is a weakness. Humility is seen by the world as a weakness, so meekness is even more looked down on by many people. Meekness is understood as kindness and gentleness. In a world of cutthroat competition and the striving to be the best, the concept of meekness is the opposite of a truly successful person. The meek person is the example of the surrendered life. The third step in the path to sanctification and the holy life is seen in the life of a meek individual. Showing compassion is not the evidence of this step toward sanctification, but living a compassionate life toward others becomes the hallmark of an example of Christ-like living.

Moving from repentance to meekness is not much of a stretch when the attitude of the heart is involved. Remember, the first step in a spiritually powerful life begins with humility. One must empty themselves of selfish attitude and lifestyle to even consider standing at the feet of Jesus Christ. Repentance, then, is the point at which a person has consciously looked deep into their heart in total abandonment of their own fleshly desires. They do this with the desire to reach up for Christ to take them by the hand and save them from themselves.

In this chapter, the idea of meekness becomes the power of God. The point at which a person evidences their true relationship with Christ is manifested in this step toward the sanctified life. Unlike humility, which is an inward evidence of personal humiliation toward repentance. Meekness is an outward evidence of a life that is in a process of spiritual growth on the path of sanctification. Therefore, the life process can be extremely difficult and, at times, unbearable. But, God's grace is sufficient for all the needs of those who truly love Him.

1. MEEKNESS: LOVE AND PATIENCE BEFORE ACTION

Give to everyone who asks of you. And from him who takes away your goods do not ask them back. And just as you want men to do to you, you also do to them likewise.   (Luke 6:30-31)

The acts committed toward each other set the stage for the way we want to be treated. The Holy Spirit serves as a conscience for the truly committed Christian Believer. Free will, however, gives them the choice to choose to follow the leading of the Spirit. Meekness is a natural outflow of the work of the Holy Spirit in the life of the Believer. The reflection of the acts of the Son of God in the flesh is shown in the individual who exhibits love, patience and kindness toward others. Jesus was the example of this in His acts toward everyone He encountered. Meekness is looked upon, today, as a weakness. But, as a follower of Jesus Christ, it is the result of a humble and repentant heart. The closer a person gets to a relationship solely committed to Christ the more these evidences will be known by others. In many church circles, the ideas of humility and meekness are not thought to possess great leadership characteristics. But, in truth, they are the highest qualities that should be sought after in a leader. A leader in a church, business, community or even a country is best as a person in service to their people and not to their ambitions.

The true leadership of God's people is pro-active and not re-active to workings of the Body of Believers and the needs of the community. Jesus is the pure example of all that is meek and humble. Most of all, He is the focus of the spiritual growth toward maturity in a life of holiness and a relationship with the Lord God. Jesus spoke to the point concerning the importance of meekness to the idea of greatness in the kingdom of God. *And He sat down, called the twelve, and said to them, "If anyone desires to be first, he shall be last of all and servant of all."* (Mark 9:35). Love and patience sets the pace for the meek mentality of the Believer in Christ. A meek person is one with a servant's heart and a heart reaching toward a viable and growing relationship with God.

2. Meekness: A Fruit of the Holy Spirit

> *But the fruit of the Spirit is love, joy, peace, longsuffering, kindness, goodness, faithfulness, gentleness, self-control. Against such there is no law.* (Galatians 5:22-23)

The fruits of the Spirit are also evidences of the manifestations of the same Spirit. Each of the fruits demonstrates a different life than the Believer had previously to their relationship with Christ. Within this list, all are characteristics of meekness.

There was a movement in the church that began in the late seventies and early eighties toward random acts of kindness. This move toward selfless acts for others developed into the one of the most effective tools of evangelism thanks to lay people and pastors in various ministries and churches around the country. This concept formed into the core focus of the growth processes of many "mega" churches. Servant Evangelism, as this ministry is called, focuses on utilizing the fruits of the Spirit in the Christian by showing lost people the love of Christ with no strings attached. There is no recruiting and no condemning, just the love of Christ shown through random acts of kindness. It is a very disarming approach to evangelism. This means that people do not expect this even out of Christians because the concept of the Christian is hard and hypocritical to most individuals outside the church. With this idea in mind, Christ is viewed as not a loving and merciful God who sacrificed His life for that person. Instead He is viewed as a condemning judge who has no regard for humanity but focused on His own supremacy. It needs to be understood that Christ Himself did not come so that the rich and powerful will become more so. He came so that sinners may be called into righteousness. Meekness is the spiritual evidence of Christ's whole presence in the life of the true Christian as seen through the Fruits of the Spirit.

3. Meekness: Essential in Teaching

And a servant of the Lord must not quarrel but be gentle to all, able to teach, patient, in humility correcting those who are in opposition, if God perhaps will grant them repentance, so that they may know the truth, and that they may come to their senses and escape the snare of the devil, having been taken captive by him to do his will.   (2 Timothy 2:24-26)

It is said that a true teacher in any respect should remain teachable and receptive to new perspectives. This implies that a person who claims they know everything, in fact knows nothing. That once a person can no longer receive instruction, they are no longer of use to the Kingdom of God. We learn new ideas and new thoughts concerning scripture every time it is read. The Spirit of God is our teacher and if we think that we understand and know everything, especially in scripture, we are considered fools in the eyes of the Lord. To be a teacher, does not make you ruler over your students.

Jesus began His ministry by teaching those whom He chose as His disciples. Even though Jesus knew all things, He in fact taught His disciples what the Father in heaven told Him to teach, so He taught with humility and meekness. He was kind to everyone and truly able to teach people from where they were spiritually, emotionally, without any regard for status. The methods used by Christ to teach were through lecture, facilitation, parables and demonstration. He demonstrated by physically, emotionally and visually showing examples as to the best ways to approach certain groups of people. Through these methods, the disciple could see the concepts He was showing them from several different perspectives and the effectiveness on different types of people. He gently instructed those around Him as well as those who opposed Him so that all would have an opportunity for repentance. Jesus Christ was the best example of meekness in the character of a teacher.

In understanding a very misunderstood word, one must first go to its beginnings for us as Greek students. Meekness as a term in the Greek New Testament from the original writings of the various authors, is derived from the Greek word *praeis*. In English, this word is translated as meekness and the modern understanding is equated with weakness. Alongside of humility, the word meekness is one of the most powerful terms to use, as well as the most complementary, concerning a Christian.

It is difficult, almost impossible, for the spirit of humanity to be meek or humble because of the stain of sin on the soul. It is only through the power of the Holy Spirit that these manifestations can be witnessed in the life of the individual. In the life of a teacher, meekness is truly important. It begins to break down barriers between the teacher and student that are normally built. In the teacher, pride and arrogant overconfidence overwhelms the student and forces them into a defensive posture of rejecting the teaching. A teacher must enter in with a teachable, meek, humble, and confident spirit. The whole idea of random acts of kindness and gentleness do filter down into every aspect of life and reflects the Spirit of God at work in the individual who does His will. Jesus Christ, as a man, set the perfect example of a teacher and how Godly meekness plays an important role in growth and development of both the teacher and the student.

4. Meekness: Essential for Hearing

Most assuredly, I say to you, he who hears My word and believes in Him who sent Me has everlasting life,

and shall not come into judgment,
but has passed from death into life.   (John 5:24)

For the Believer in Jesus Christ to understand and believe, they must hear the word spoken. They must not just hear with their ears but essentially with their heart. A person hurried in all their ways and who does not slow down to wait and listen for the Lord will never learn the truths of God. A meek person is one who is patient, gentle and slow to speak. Human nature is driven toward a fast-paced life that is hallmarked by the idea of "shoot first and ask questions later." With this mentality, it is a wonder that anything is ever accomplished in an orderly manner. Because we are more righteous than that guy, we hold all the answers. And if we hold all the answers, then what do we have to listen to? We know it all! Right!

A very important component in the life of the Christian is to be different. God told His people that they are "a peculiar people set apart by God to be holy." In other words, we are not to be like everybody else, we are to be different. Christians should be reflections of Christ to the world. How can a person be meek and not be a good listener? One who is slow to speak and quick to listen.

The terms into which we have chosen to live a Christian life, finds at its core Christ-likeness. Jesus was a patient, kind, and gentle man, and through Him listening to the cries of His people, we understand more that He demonstrated in His life. His patience, mercy and kindness was where He set an example, this is true. But, His all-knowing presence set Him apart. He knew when people were hurting and when they just needed an ear and an open heart.

When people are at the bottom of their ladder and are struggling with life, it is then that the Holy Spirit not only gives them the strength but also will climb the ladder with them. The Holy Spirit opens the ears of the individual and allows them to hear what the Lord has for them to hear. As a person sets aside their strong, tainted, sinful will and allows God's will be done in their lives, then the Holy Spirit is given opportunity to open the hearing of one who loves the Lord. It is a wonderful new world that is found beyond the human sinful will. If we would only allow the Holy Spirit into our lives, then the new and greatest adventures would begin.

A true servant of Christ has yielded themselves and their will to that of God and the mighty work of the Holy Spirit. The manifestation of the yielding to the Spirit and servant attitude is true meekness or Godly meekness. This is not weakness but strength beyond your greatest understanding.

5. MEEKNESS: PRECIOUS IN GOD'S SIGHT

> *But you are a chosen generation, a royal priesthood, a holy nation, His own special people, that you may proclaim the praises of Him who called you out of darkness into His marvelous light; who once were not a people but are now the people of God, who had not obtained mercy but now have obtained mercy.*
> (1Peter 2:9-10)

One thing is obvious in a person with the Holy Spirit at work in their lives is that they exhibit a pure and true form of meekness. This begins the true mark of Christ-like character. This is precious in God's sight. It is this characteristic that caused King David to be called a "man after God's own heart." It is evident in the countenance of a person that has the Holy Spirit as their sole provider. When we stand before the Father in heaven, I for one want to hear Him say "well done good and faithful servant, come into your rest set for you from the beginning of the world." A person who claims allegiance to you but does what they want even though it is opposite of what you see as right is not a person who cares about you. You are precious in the eyes of the Lord! God is in love, deep love, more intimate love than you can imagine, with *you*! When it is said that you are precious in God's sight, it is much more passionate and deep than you can define with words. He gave His life to save your eternal soul. That is inconceivable with human understanding. Therefore, a person must focus entirely on Christ and Him alone.

What do you think the Lord feels like when a person pledges their allegiance to Him and prays on occasion, then turns and does their own thing contrary to what the Lord told them was best for them? You are precious to Him, but you also must realize that Jesus Christ has always been the same yesterday, today and forever. He never changes how He feels about you, but He becomes disappointed with you. Just as when the disobedience of a child is disappointing to a parent or distancing yourself from your spouse is destructive to the relationship, so it is with our relationship with Christ.

Meekness is the manifestation of the Holy Presence in the life of the Christian that truly says to others around you that the Holy Spirit is real in you. As I have said before, it is a gift to be a good person. But it is a spiritual gift to be a person characterized by others as meek, gentle and kind. Even though meekness is only the third step in the process of growth called sanctification. As you strive toward glorification, meekness is a crucial step to the beginning of developing your relationship with Christ. No relationship ever just happens. Jesus Christ understands that a human individual must be disrupted and counteract a lifetime of sin and misunderstanding. It is a process and not a onetime event. Yes! You are precious in God's sight! God's sight is that much clearer when a person enters this level of relationship. This is true of their relationship with God and with all others around them. The old man has died and is being resurrected into a new man. Glory to God for His patience!

WHERE DO WE GO FROM HERE?

Meekness in today's world is not to be the understanding of those worshiping Christ. You have learned that the world views meekness as weakness and this opens the committed Christian up to persecution. Meekness, in its purest form, has at the base patience, love, kindness and gentleness. Against any of these there are no laws.

The beauty found within the concept of meekness is the Believer's view of the world around them. They may not be part of the world, but they are in the world. Jesus, through the work of the Holy Spirit, gives the meek Believer a new view of reality and therefore, a Christ-like attitude toward even their enemies.

> *But made Himself of no reputation,*
> *taking the form of a bondservant,*
> *and coming in the likeness of men.*
> *And being found in appearance as a man,*
> *He humbled Himself*
> *and became obedient to the point of death,*
> *even the death of the cross.* (Philippians 2:7-8)

The meek Christian must take the mind of Christ and view their surroundings through the eyes of Christ. Your understanding of the meek Christ must be where you place your trust. Otherwise, there will be judgment and condemnation in your heart. You will never be able to have the mind of Christ apart from the work of the Holy Spirit. Continue the race in meekness set before you in the power of the Holy Spirit and He will guide your steps.

CLOSING PRAYER:

Most gracious and loving Father, help me in patience, love, and kindness be all You want me to be. Forgive my sinful tendencies and cleanse me from all unrighteousness. May I see the world through the eyes of Christ and approach those in the world with meekness and gentleness. In Jesus' Name, Amen.

DISCUSSION QUESTIONS

Meekness Before God

1. How is meekness considered a powerful strength in your walk with Christ?

2. Why is it important to have meekness to outwardly express love and patience to others?

3. In what ways is meekness essential to growth and living as followers of Christ?

4. How does the power of meekness help us to be Christians?

5

EAGERLY SEEKING ALL THAT
GOD WANTS TO OFFER

SPIRITUAL DESIRE

Blessed are those who hunger and thirst for righteousness, for they shall be filled. (Matthew 5:6)

The desire to be closer and more intimate with the living God of creation is a natural outflow of the real work of the Spirit of God in the life of the individual. By this stage in the growth toward sanctification, there is an overwhelming need or even hunger for the things of God. This is the point where the newness of that single experience of the conversion moment, when we surrendered our lives into His hands, is now coupled with intense spiritual desire. Think of it as you would a personal relationship with someone you truly care about and want to please. All you want to do is please that person no matter what it takes; and your desire is for them and them alone. You would give up your lifestyle to spend another moment with them. Well, this is the way it is with our relationship with Jesus Christ. The Holy Spirit is the catalyst through which we build that relationship with the living sinless God. Humans by their very nature are sinful and God cannot stand the presence of sin.

It is the work of the Holy Spirit in the life of the individual that assists them to press on past that tainted nature into the open arms of a loving and merciful God. The closer you get to Jesus Christ and a relationship with Him, the more your desire grows. Just like in a relationship with a person you dearly love. The more you learn, the more you love. The difference is that Jesus is the lover of your heart, but even more than this, He is the lover of your soul. He wants to spend eternity with you. He chose to physically and spiritually lay down His own life so that you may be with Him forever. There is no human relationship that can say this in truth. As we take a closer look at the spiritual desire, more precisely spiritual hunger and thirst, of the individual, there needs to be considered that the human condition is corrupt. God understands this and chooses to love you anyway.

SPIRITUAL DESIRE: SEEKING OF THE SOUL

As the deer pants for the water brooks,
So pants my soul for You, O God.
My soul thirsts for God, for the living God.
When shall I come and appear before God? (Psalm 42:1-2)

In this passage of scripture, the author begins by acknowledging the depravity of their own soul. Lost and wretched a soul you may possess but a deeper, whiter soul you seek. A person, no matter how lost, will find God through Jesus Christ in the power of the Holy Spirit, if they truly seek Him with all their heart and especially their soul. Jesus said in Matthew 6:33, "But, seek you first His kingdom and His righteousness, and all these things will be given to you as well." The priority of putting God first in the life of the individual is the key to the kingdom of God and a true pure relationship with Jesus Christ. Just as in any relationship, a person must first seek Him. Everyone says, "I am waiting on them to make the first move." This is the attitude of a person who is not willing to commit whole-heartedly to the relationship. But, a person who goes out of their way to show their love for the individual is one who truly shows desire for that person. Jesus Christ never leaves you. He said this countless times. The *person* separates themselves from the love of God. It is God who remains with open arms ready to receive the one that was lost.

King Solomon in all his glory sought for wisdom from God. In the council of God to Solomon, He gave Solomon four simple objectives that He wanted His people to achieve (2 Chronicles 7:14). First, He told them to humble themselves. Be before Him in total reverence and worship Him alone. Second, He told His people to pray. God wanted to establish communication with His people. Third, He wanted His people to seek Him with all their heart, mind and soul. He wanted to be first and foremost in the lives of His people. As David said, "as a deer pants for water, so my soul pants after You O God."

We are not playing a child's game of hide and seek. We are not hiding for God to find us. God knows where we are hiding. It is He who is lost to us because we are not seeking Him. He has never left the spot where we walked away from Him. The fourth objective God proposed to Solomon and His people was that they turn from their wicked ways. Well, if you truly humbled yourself, fervently praying and sought out a relationship with God with all your heart, mind and soul, then chances are the spirit within that gives witness to God's Spirit would have no choice but to turn from its wicked ways. This is not always true with everyone.

The key to understanding this is to realize the idea of human nature. Human nature has as its veil, sin. Therefore, the otherwise pure created nature becomes the sinful nature. Since sin entered the world with Adam and Eve, God has shown His love in many ways to His creation. But, the biggest nemesis to God reconciling a relationship, was His greatest gift, free will. People make choices, every moment of everyday. Each decision forms the path an individual carves out for themselves for their lives. The positive side of free will is that they have the opportunity make the right choices which would in turn steer them down the better or even the best path. The Holy Spirit at work in the life of the individual erases the gray areas. He enlightens the paths for those who are eagerly seeking a relationship with Jesus Christ.

The eternal mortality of an individual is found in the way that the soul is nourished. The Psalms speak much to desire of the soul toward a singularly focused relationship and the way that the condition of the soul dictates the actions of the individual. How do we know if we are truly saved? What is first in your life and what is the first thing you do upon waking in morning? If both are answered with seeking God, then you are on the right track. If not, then you need to turn and begin seeking Him. The sinful nature is difficult to rid yourself of, but through the power of the Holy Spirit and seeking the presence of God, it can be accomplished.

Psalm 34:15 states that "The eyes of the Lord are on the righteous and His ears are attentive to their cry." Psalm 92:12 says that "The righteous will flourish like a palm tree, they will grow like the cedar of Lebanon." The main point to understand is that the Lord is our God and He wants to be the one that we focus on in life. He wants to be the focus of all that we do. The righteousness of God is the source of growth and strength that is needed to become a true servant and warrior of the Living God. An individual cannot serve and worship God if they are directing their soul to another love. Jesus Christ in His address to the churches in and around Ephesus said that the only thing He had against them was that they had forgotten their first love. In other translations, the word "forgotten" is also understood as "forsaken." The word forsaken has much more consequences and carries with it the idea of total rejection or turning away from a person. Jesus said this as one of His last statements while hanging from the cross, "Father why have you forsaken me?" This is a strong statement. For Jesus at His moment of suffering and dying, it was a real experience. Jesus had the sins of the whole world resting on Him.

He knew the cost of your redemption. At that moment, Jesus, the only begotten Son of God, saw God's presence turn away because God cannot look upon sin. It is when an individual comes to the point that Jesus did in His last breath when He said, "into your hands I commend my Spirit," that they are truly seeking after the righteousness of God.

SPIRITUAL RIGHTEOUS: THE RIGHTEOUSNESS OF GOD

The LORD is righteous in all His ways,
Gracious in all His works. (Psalm 145:17)

One of the main notions of the work of God is that when Jesus Christ ascended to the throne of God the Father, the Holy Spirit was sent to be the guide and strength for those who sought after Him and wanted that relationship with the Living God. God is not only righteous, but He is the righteousness that we seek. Apart from the righteousness of God, there would be no redemption, no resurrection, no forgiveness of sin. It is because of God's unconditional love toward His creation that we as mere humans can have a relationship with our creator. More to the point, it is in His love for us that we are even given the opportunity to seek His righteousness. And it is through His love and righteousness that the Holy Spirit works in the life of those who seek Him. A person cannot find anything that they are not seeking. If there is one thing for sure, the desire for righteousness begins to grow the moment you begin to seek the righteousness of God. So, in reflecting on verse 17 from Psalm 145, a person needs to evaluate their passion. Is their passion for a relationship with Jesus Christ and focus on Him alone or is it a "need-based" relationship?

Focus on the Holy Spirit, the gift from God, for help and guidance. This is the gift of God for the righteousness that is sought. The gift of the Holy Spirit is the vehicle by which He is speaking directly to and through His people. The "need-based" relationship is when the individual only goes to the Lord in times of trouble. If a person seeks nothing but the righteousness of God, they will find it anytime. When in Matthew 6:33 Jesus says that you should "seek first the Kingdom of God and His righteousness and all these things will be added unto you," He means it. Understanding the righteousness of God is not required to have that relationship. But seek Him and His righteousness first and all you desire within the Will of God will be given to you.

BEING IMITATORS OF CHRIST:
THE RIGHTEOUSNESS OF CHRIST

For I say to you, that unless your righteousness exceeds the righteousness of the scribes and Pharisees, you will by no means enter the kingdom of heaven. (Matthew 5:20)

Seeking the righteousness of Christ is stepping into a world that few travel. The journey is challenging at times but truly rewarding for those who are seeking Him with all their heart. When someone thirsts and hungers for the righteousness of Christ, they tend to be rejected and ridiculed by those who don't understand. But, you are to be imitators of Christ and through those experiences you are more than conquerors. Looking at this verse in Matthew, there can be seen a reflection of this same implication today with "Scholars," "Bishops," "Pastors," "church leaders," and the list goes on. There is no need to spend too much time "beating a dead horse." Jesus is telling Christians that you need to surpass all the so called "experts" and "righteous or pious ones." Much of their "righteousness" is found in status and power. Jesus said that He came not to be served but to serve. The work of the Holy Spirit is to point and guide the individual Believer to a pure walk of service to God. The true righteousness of Christ can only be found through the work of the Holy Spirit.

The early church suffered a great turmoil following the time of the Apostles. The acts, teachings, and many of the writings of the Apostles served as powerful witnesses to the power of the Holy Spirit in the individual and the Body of Believers. But, as time went by, the teachings of Christ that were held as sacred by the Apostles, were twisted and distorted when human ideals were being introduced into pure Christian teachings. The Spirit of God was replaced with that of man. The Church came to the point of ruling countries; becoming corrupt to persecuting and killing Christians for the sake of power and control. It was not until the Protestant Reformation and those who stood up in the power of the Holy Spirit that the Church began to look to God once again.

When the world becomes more appealing to the Christian than a personal relationship with Jesus Christ, the Church begins to intertwine worldly rational thought into Christian belief and this leads to justification to most any act in the name of Jesus. This is wrong and the Spirit of God, the Holy Spirit, is not a part of it.

GODLINESS: RIGHTEOUSNESS INTO HOLINESS

> *Therefore I exhort first of all that supplications, prayers, inter-cessions, and giving of thanks be made for all men, for kings and all who are in authority, that we may lead a quiet and peaceable life in all godliness and reverence.* (1 Timothy 2:1-2)

When searching for the righteousness of Christ through the power of the Holy Spirit, the search for a life of peace and wholeness is the general priority for most Christians. The pursuit of holiness and godliness, at its very core, is seen more clearly the more a person narrows their focus on Christ alone. The beauty of loving God is found in the relationship sought. The idea of holiness cannot be understood apart from two things.

First, the person eagerly seeking out Christ where everything else falls away and nothing else matters to the individual but pursuing the relationship. Second, that the Holy Spirit, the Spirit of God, finds the connection with the one searching and fuels the search. We all desire to live a peaceful existence. But, the reality of it all is that life must be lived. Unless we become narrow-minded Believers focused only on Christ and His love, our hope for this peace is lost to the world and all that it offers.

> *But reject profane and old wives' fables, and exercise yourself toward godliness. For bodily exercise profits a little, but godliness is profitable for all things, having promise of the life that now is and of that which is to come.* (1 Timothy 4:7-8)

Gossip and slanderous speech has no place in the life of the faithful Believer. If the fruit of the Spirit of God is not evidenced in the life of the person claiming to be of God, then they are a liar and the truth is not in them. The argument for the beauty of the fit physical body is that it is the temple of the Holy Spirit and we should maintain it accordingly. But, Paul is saying to Timothy that though physical fitness is of value to the body in this life, godliness stands paramount to all things because it affects things to eternity. He also drives the point even further in saying that godliness holds the promise of the life in the Spirit from the present time you received into the eternal rest. When a person equates the beauty of the body with godliness then godliness has been overcome with vanity. The human nature is known to be corrupt and sinful. This is true until the person surrenders to the love and mercy of Christ. Then, it is through the power of the Holy Spirit that God begins the lifelong process of molding the Believer like a lump of clay ready to be formed.

Godliness or holiness is something eagerly sought after and is the true evidence of the person who is truly hungering and thirsting for the righteousness of God. Their value is found in what God thinks of them and not what the world thinks. Paul continues in his charge to Timothy in 1 Timothy 6:11, "But you, O man of God, flee these things and pursue righteousness, godliness, faith, love, patience, gentleness." He is charging Timothy to remain in pursuit of godliness and holiness.

All the things of God are golden in comparison to that of the world. The world offers nothing but corruption and death. Even within churches and among so called "Believers" there is controversy and strife. For it is only in the power of the Holy Spirit toward living the holy, godly life that true peace is possible. Paul once again sums up the pursuit to godliness in his letter to Titus when he says,

> For the grace of God that brings salvation has appeared to all men, teaching us that, denying ungodliness and worldly lusts, we should live soberly, righteously, and godly in the present age, looking for the blessed hope and glorious appearing of our great God and Savior Jesus Christ, who gave Himself for us, that He might redeem us from every lawless deed and purify for Himself His own special people, zealous for good works.

> *Speak these things, exhort, and rebuke with all authority. Let*
> *no one despise you.* (Titus 2:11-15)

To bring to a point, it is our eager and earnest pursuit after the righteousness of God where we can find that which our spirit desires more than anything. A holy relationship with the Living God in Christ through the power of the Holy Spirit is our desire and as we grow into holiness, it is His righteousness we seek.

WHERE DO WE GO FROM HERE?

The real evidence is found in the noticeable change in one's life. The Holy Spirit at work in the life of an individual is seen in the fruit produced. If, in fact, the individual is eagerly seeking after the righteousness of God then they will either repel or draw others in to God's presence. People will want what you have and desire to know more about what is different.

The one who hungers and thirsts for the righteousness of God is completely and totally committed to the ways and will of God. The beauty of this righteousness is that it is a transforming work of the mind and heart.

> *And do not be conformed to this world, but be transformed*
> *by the renewing of your mind, that you may prove what is that*
> *good and acceptable and perfect will of God.* (Romans 12:2)

Remember that with the transforming of the mind comes a power and drive that is unmatched. When you focus on the striving for the glory and righteousness of God and seek first the Kingdom, the Holy Spirit will be more able to guide and empower you. The Apostle Paul goes on to say concerning the desire for the righteousness of God,

> *Therefore do not let your good be spoken of as evil; for the*
> *kingdom of God is not eating and drinking, but righteousness and*
> *peace and joy in the Holy Spirit. For he who serves Christ in these*
> *things is acceptable to God and approved by men.*
> (Romans 14:16-18)

As the one who is striving to be like Jesus in all aspects of life, you should consider that you really look to God for the path and not to the world. Focus on Jesus for answers. You can only maintain the focus in the power and leadership of the Spirit of God to light the way. When you eagerly desire the things of God and His righteousness, the eyes of your heart will be open to the call of God through the empowerment of the Holy Spirit.

CLOSING PRAYER:

Heavenly Father, I know You are my God and Savior. Cleanse me from all unrighteousness that I may seek Your face and find You and Your righteousness. For it is to Your Glory that I hunger and thirst for your ways and Your righteousness. In Jesus Name, Amen.

QUESTIONS FOR DISCUSSION

Spiritual Desire for God

1. As you grow closer to a relationship with Christ, how does this affect the desires in your life?

2. Our understanding of righteousness differs from that of God. The more we seek and desire Him our needs should also change. How and why?

3. The closer we grow toward him the more we want to grow closer. Shouldn't the aim be to be imitators and not just spectators of the Will of God?

4. As the righteousness you seek prompts you to grow closer, does this not lead you in the next step toward Holiness before a Holy God?

6

HAVING THE HEART OF CHRIST
TOWARD THE LOST

Blessed are the merciful,
For they shall obtain mercy.　　　　　　　　(Matthew 5:7)

As the list of character attributes becomes more evident in the life of a growing Christian, one should start to see a real change in the thinking and actions. *Mercy* is one of those attributes of the true Believer in Christ that begins to set the faith of that person apart from the rest. Many people, even in the churches, merely go through the motions of Christianity. In the life of this reborn Christian, they begin to see the lost and dying world through the eyes of Christ. They have a new perspective and not with disgust through the judgmental eyes of the humanistic "Christian." The Christian who merely goes through the motions of Christianity is one who seems to be the active person. This person is involved in everything and makes every attempt to be involved to feed a need to be accepted by that society. They are "Social Butterflies" and tend to use the church as their social spot to spread and gather gossip.

The next person is the one who chooses to be accepted by the fact that they just show up every time the doors of the church are open. They are not active in the same way as the social butterfly. The activity they choose is to be what is affectionately called a pew person or pew sitter. They show up in church just to make sure they are recognized by the important ones. They have done their part for the Lord. Most of the time, they are great tithers and at times make sure people know it. The last but not the least of the groups of attendees are those who just sneak in and sit hoping not to be noticed. At times, they tend to be fashionably late but they are usually not unnoticed by the pastor or even a deacon or charter member. They choose to be unnoticed and they believe that if they just show up that God will be pleased and mark them present in His book. But, as it turns out the only book that they are checked off in is the one that posts the number of those present that day.

All this rambling is to prove a point as to the importance of being active for the Lord. Among the three groups mentioned, they make up more than 80% of most mainline churches. The final 20% are those who are trying to please God as much as they are able. About 10% of that group is easily distracted but do mission projects for outreach to the lost because they see it as their duty and it says so in scripture. The final 2% to 10%, it varies from church to church, is solely committed to the work of the Lord to the lost and is burning out in ministry because of the lack of support. Most people in the church will throw loads of money at projects if they believe in it strongly enough. But, very few will commit to service for the Lord. They believe that their monetary gift is their service. The money is needed, true. But, Jesus said that He came to serve and not be served. In the Great Commission, Jesus was speaking to all Christians. He wasn't just speaking to those who say they feel called into that type of ministry, He called everybody.

In Romans Chapter 12 verse two, the Apostle Paul says that the Believer should be transformed by the renewing of the mind. This means that we should have the mind of Christ and with the mind of Christ we will view the world around us in a more sobering light. It does not mean to get involved in the world and be more a part of it. Showing mercy is addressed by Paul as a gift of the Holy Spirit and therefore believes it is imparted on certain people. Mercy shown to others should be a natural outflow from a heart totally committed to the work of Christ. "Blessed are the merciful for they will be shown mercy." If a person shows mercy to another, then their reward lies in the blessed hands of the Lord. The flip side of that implies that if you don't show mercy then why should you expect mercy in return.

DIVINE MERCY: ETERNAL AND UNDESERVED

As a father pities his children,
So the LORD pities those who fear Him.
For He knows our frame;
He remembers that we are dust.   (Psalm 103:13-14)

Humans, regardless of their status, do not deserve mercy from the God and Creator of all things. The human creature is a mere speck on the time line of eternity. Yet, our Creator desires a loving, personal relationship with us. He loves all people of the world as a father loves a child. Jesus refers to Him as the Father on many occasions. For two millennia, the fingers have been pointing blame always to someone else, never to themselves. The Jews are blame, the High Priest and the Jewish leaders are the ones who arranged to have him put to death, right? Sure, they had a hand in it, but what about those who were in the crowds screaming insults and spitting on him on the *Via Dolorosa*? Or, those who were among the multitudes that heard Him speak and were witnesses to the miracles? What about the Roman soldiers who flogged Him to the point of being unrecognizable and within an inch of death? What about Judas Iscariot who betrayed our Lord for a mere thirty pieces of silver?

From there let us look to the disciples themselves, they fled under the fear of suffering the same fate. And, except for John, Mary Magdalen, and His mother Mary, they are never heard from until after His resurrection? What about Christians today, who stand up in church and profess Jesus as Lord one minute and leave the church only to curse the driver who pulled in front of them moments later. Yes, God the Father and the Son have mercy on those who eagerly seek Him. The key words are "eagerly seek." So, let us try again at pointing the finger of blame for the death of our

Lord. Regardless to who accused Him falsely or even the ones who drove the nails into His feet and hands.

All of humanity are to blame, both past and present, for the death of our Savior. But, God alone is responsible for raising His Son from the dead. It is God alone who is merciful enough to allow His Only Son to die for the disgusting sins of humanity.

> *As for man, his days are like grass;*
> *As a flower of the field, so he flourishes.*
> *For the wind passes over it, and it is gone,*
> *And its place remembers it no more.*
> *But the mercy of the LORD is from everlasting to everlasting*
> *On those who fear Him,*
> *And His righteousness to children's children,*
> *To such as keep His covenant,*
> *And to those who remember*
> *His commandments to do them.*   (Psalm 103:15-18)

Divine eternal understanding of mercy is beyond the grasp of the human mind. It is unfathomable for anyone to even relate to the mercy shown toward a sinful, prideful, and arrogant people. He set the example through the birth, life and death of His Son, Jesus Christ. This was the only way for humanity, in their fallen depraved state, to have an opportunity for reconciliation back into a relationship with God. It is only through God's divine mercy that a person can be saved from certain eternal death.

Humanity's days are numbered on the linear time line of eternity. The lives of individuals making a difference barely makes a ripple, but God is the only constant in all eternity. Remember that the God of eternity is the One who shows true Love and Mercy. For those who fear Him and choose to follow Him, they are shown divine mercy. This is the mercy that sees the big picture and, despite our rejection of Him, He chooses to have mercy and show an unconditional Love toward us.

DIVINE MERCY: ENCOURAGES SINNERS TO REPENTANCE

So, rend your heart, and not your garments;
Return to the LORD your God,
For He is gracious and merciful,
Slow to anger, and of great kindness;
And He relents from doing harm. (Joel 2:13)

When a person returns to the Lord, they have made a change. They make a change that renders sin repulsive to them just as God is repulsed by sin. Once a Believer, who is totally committed to the work of the Lord becomes committed in their heart, this commitment, by its very nature, tends to show mercy towards others. The mercy expressed should not be shown out of an obligation, but out of a true unconditional love toward another fellow sinner.

The committed merciful Believer is now seeing the world around them through the eyes of Christ. This in turn gives a new perception of the Believer in their relationship with the one they are ministering too. This person will talk and act differently toward everything and everybody. Their perception of the world around them changes because Jesus has taken away the scales of sin that clouded their view of humanity. Therefore, they are guided by their attitude and temperament toward others. Through the example of the merciful servant of God, there is a stirring and desire seen by a lost person that directs them toward Christ and His love. People want something better. The soul within the person knows and groans for the connection with the living Spirit of God.

In this same understanding, it needs to be noted that because of the overwhelming unconditional love poured out by God the Father, the Believer will experience forgiveness of sins. The forgiveness of sins, being at the base of the Christian Believer's life, has at its core the realization of divine mercy. God showing mercy toward a lost creation and world is the example set for the everyday person who is a follower of Christ. Christians are called to know and do for those less fortunate. Not only the less fortunate, but for all people and for all time. The prophet Micah states:

Who is a God like You, pardoning iniquity
And passing over the transgression
of the remnant of His heritage?
He does not retain His anger forever,
Because He delights in mercy.   (Micah 7:18)

The whole foundation of mercy is viewed in the acts of God toward those who love and seek that relationship with Him. Micah is telling the Believer that God not only likes showing mercy, but He delights and thoroughly enjoys when He can show mercy toward His people. The flip side of this is that God is also just with the pardoning and forgiveness of sin. When a person, a sinner forgiven or not, seeks His face and truly turn from their wicked ways, He forgives but that does not excuse us from the consequences of the sin.

David, being "a man after God's own heart," sinned several great sins before God. He committed adultery, murder, coveted his neighbor's wife, and the list of commandments broken goes on. But David honestly sought redemption before God for all counts. He sought God's mercy for all that he had done. It had all started with one event and it just snowballed into a massive heap of sin. David was called "a man after God's own heart" not for the great things that he accomplished but because of his great love and commitment toward God. God showed David mercy, but it was served on the plate of justice. There were consequences to David's actions and it stood as a reminder for him to constantly remember his need for God. He learned that he was never beyond the long arm of God's justice along with the gentle arm of His mercy.

Mary the mother of Jesus recognized God's divine mercy as she was praising Him following the announcement to Elizabeth of the forthcoming birth of her glorious son whose Father is God.

And His mercy is on those who fear Him
From generation to generation.
He has shown strength with His arm;
He has scattered the proud
in the imagination of their hearts.

He has put down the mighty from their thrones,
And exalted the lowly.
He has filled the hungry with good things,
And the rich He has sent away empty.
He has helped His servant Israel,
In remembrance of His mercy,
As He spoke to our fathers,
To Abraham and to his seed forever.   (Luke 1:50-55)

Mary understood God's mercy. It was not for her alone, but for all humanity, past, present and future. The divine mercy of God is glorious in the fact that He even grants mercy to such a depraved and fallen world. But just as the love of God is unconditional so is the mercy of God unconditional. Otherwise, fallen humanity could not truly understand the consequences of falling into the deep pit of sin without the possibility of forgiveness or mercy.

The Apostle Paul gives the Believer an excellent summary of where gratitude should be given because of the fallen state of humanity in his letter to the Ephesians:

among whom also we all once conducted ourselves in the lusts of
our flesh, fulfilling the desires of the flesh and of the mind, and
were by nature children of wrath,
 just as the others.

But God, who is rich in mercy, because of His great love with
which He loved us, even when we were dead in trespasses, made
us alive together with Christ
(by grace you have been saved),   (Ephesians 2:3-5)

Paul experienced, and truly realized, the true mercy of God standing alongside the sinful depraved condition of an undeserving creation. Humanity does not deserve the grace, love and mercy of Almighty God. Humanity did not deserve for God to come down from His throne in heaven, to become as low as a servant, to live and die a criminal's death. God, at the point of the death of Jesus, turned His back on the sin that was with Jesus on the cross. He could have turned His back away from His creation. But, what makes God more merciful is His love and His grace toward His people.

God's Commandment: Show Mercy

He has shown you, O man, what is good;
And what does the LORD require of you
But to do justly, to love mercy,
And to walk humbly with your God?   (Micah 6:8)

What is my purpose in life? That is a question asked by all people at some point in their lives. They can only answer the question based on their relationships and experiences. What is their relationship with the world? What is their relationship to one another? Or, what, if any, is their relationship with God? Even a better question is: "What is their god?" The prophet Micah states plainly that the Lord simply requires or commands a lover of God to "act justly, love mercy and walk humbly with their God."

Let us look at each one. First, the Believer or lover of God must "act justly." Then ask the question, to whom should I act justly? The obvious answer is to act justly toward *all* people. Because when you act justly toward a sinner in the world, you have set the stage for their salvation. Second, Micah said that the lover of God must "love mercy." The question here is how does a person love mercy? It is not the act of loving mercy for its own sake. It is to this point that mercy becomes the cornerstone of your relationships with others through the power of God's Holy Spirit. This is when God's true unconditional love is evidenced. Lastly, it is only because of God's unconditional mercy that a person can walk "humbly" with their God. Adam and Eve, before the Fall, walked and talked with the Lord God in the Garden of Eden. They walked humbly and with a pure innocence. This is what God wants for His people. In James' letter, he tells the Believer that mercy triumphs over judgment and is shown through the speech and actions of His people.

> *So, speak and so do as those who will be judged by the law of*
> *liberty. For judgment is without mercy*
> *to the one who has shown no mercy.*
> *Mercy triumphs over judgment.* (James 2:12-13)

Because of the fallen state and condition of sinful humanity, the first reaction is to issue judgment. God gave humanity a perfect example of mercy personified in the body of Jesus of Nazareth. It is through the Spirit of Christ, God's Spirit, that a person can show mercy toward another individual, just out of unconditional love. The Holy Spirit is the way through which a person is enabled to show mercy.

In Proverbs 3, the author is setting the foundation upon which a person can grow into a deeper relationship through the power of the Holy Spirit. Toward which a person will show acts of mercy as a normal action.

> *Let not mercy and truth forsake you;*
> *Bind them around your neck,*
> *write them on the tablet of your heart,* (Proverbs 3:3)

Remember that God's mercy is more than anyone truly deserves and the Holy Spirit is there for strength and hope. Unconditional love and true faithfulness should be at the basis for unconditional acts of mercy toward a lost and dying world for their salvation.

WHERE DO WE GO FROM HERE?

Mercy, and the act of showing mercy, is the outpouring of the love of God toward those whom He loves. It is because the Christian has the love of God in them that mercy and compassion is expressed. Everything to this point in our study has been focused on the subjective or inner growth of the Believer. Now, with mercy, the love and compassion of God can finally be glorified and work of the Holy Spirit be evidenced.

> *Then Jesus went about all the cities and villages, teaching in*
> *their synagogues, preaching the gospel of the kingdom, and healing*

*every sickness and every disease among the people. But when He
saw the multitudes, He was moved with compassion for them, because they were weary and scattered, like sheep having no shepherd.
Then He said to His disciples, "The harvest truly is plentiful, but
the laborers are few. Therefore pray the Lord of the harvest to send
out laborers into His harvest."*   (Matthew 9:35-38)

Jesus had compassion and had shown mercy on the multitudes
and not just single individuals. Those who are lost in the world
today need the compassion shown through those who are willing
to step forward and freely give the mercy and love of God. The
harvest is plentiful but the workers are few. The ones who allow the
Holy Spirit to teach the ways and love of God toward others will in
turn guide others in the ways of mercy. Mercy is the outward act
of direct obedience to the work and guidance of the Holy Spirit.

CLOSING PRAYER:

*Father, in heaven, cleanse my mind and my heart that I may
see what You see. Help me that I may, with a clean heart show mercy
in obedience to Your love and righteousness. To the Glory of God,
and the Son through the power of the Holy Spirit.
In Jesus Name, Amen.*

QUESTIONS FOR DISCUSSION

Showing the Mercy of God

1. In your Christian walk, how would you describe the idea of
    act of mercy?

2. Understanding your position in relation to a perfectly Holy
    God, what do you believe we as humans deserve?

3. When mercy is shown to others, how do they respond? How
    does this shape your view on God?

4. Even though mercy is the natural outflow of the love of Christ, how does it help you focus even more when God gives the Command to love and show mercy to others?

7

Spiritual Vision for God's Work

Blessed are the pure in heart,
For they shall see God.   (Matthew 5:8)

Stepping into the next stage of growth and development in the life of the Christian, one must continue to look inward to the soul. This is into the soul that seeks a relationship with the Creator to see God and His will for their lives. Purifying the heart is not an easy process. It is for the person who opens their world to the total surrender of the work of the Holy Spirit. The desire is to have a clear spiritual vision for the things of God.

The Holy Spirit plays a large role in pointing the heart of the individual in the direction that God has given them to travel. The road to purification is truly one of the hardest traveled to date. It is hardest to expose one's life into a transparent hands-on vehicle for the total use of God's eternal purpose. The person experiencing this level of spiritual maturity has great insight into the world around them. There are no inhibitions in their life toward those around them because the Holy Spirit can now work as the Lord God commands. The difference from spiritual purity and the other previous stages of growth is that purity opens the veil of knowledge and vision as never experienced before. But, the crucial point comes when one truly experiences spiritual purity. Instead of being prideful or arrogant, the person experiences a depth of humility that cannot be understood except through a life connected with Jesus Christ by the Holy Spirit.

PURE IN HEART: ONE RAISED FROM SPIRITUAL DEATH

> *If then you were raised with Christ, seek those things which are above, where Christ is, sitting at the right hand of God. Set your mind on things above, not on things on the earth. For you died, and your life is hidden with Christ in God. When Christ who is our life appears, then you also will appear with Him in glory.*   (Colossians 3:1-4)

An individual who is seeking God with all their heart, mind, soul and strength is one who has died to self. The concept of dying to self is understood by the total and unrelenting change evidenced when a person has surrendered their life solely to Jesus Christ. Everyone, no matter your past circumstances, has surrendered their own will and their human nature to the Will of God to be totally committed to the work of God. At the moment a person gives their life to the Lord Jesus Christ, they are a new creation. The old person was nailed on the cross with Christ. No matter how good you were before being saved, your soul was tainted with sin and needed to die to self to allow the Holy Spirit to work a mighty work of grace.

You thought that you were good before, but watch out now! Jesus told us that He is the Way, the Truth, and the Life and that no one goes to the Father except by Him. A person who is pure in heart is one who finally and fully realizes the depraved circumstances from which they have come and recognizes that they were wretched and sinful. Yet, Jesus Christ loves them so much that He died for them. But, they are the eyes, hands and feet of Christ to a lost and dying world. You are a new creature, raised to life with Christ, who is empowered for God's service.

The mind of humanity is easily drawn away from the intended purpose that God the Father has ordained. The Apostle Paul, in his letter to the Romans, speaks to the issue of worldly influence;

> *And do not be conformed to this world, but be transformed*
> *by the renewing of your mind, that you may prove what is that*
> *good and acceptable and perfect will of God.*   (Romans 12:2)

The mind is the processor of everything that enters the body through the eyes and ears. The condition of the mind coincides with the manner of speech that a Believer portrays. If the mind is weak and takes in only negative and bad things, then it will process the negative and what comes out will be related to it. But, with a Believer who has a transformed mind, they can block that speech or what was seen and turn it into something to glorify God. Because the negative is a means by which to destroy another, it is unique to someone who is pure in heart not to destroy another. The Apostle Peter says concerning the body and the attitude of the mind,

> *Therefore, since Christ suffered for us in the flesh, arm your-*
> *selves also with the same mind, for he who has suffered in the flesh*
> *has ceased from sin, that he no longer should live the rest of his*
> *time in the flesh for the lusts of men, but for the will of God.*
>   (1Peter 4:1-2)

We are soldiers in the Army of Christ! One who is totally committed to the work of Christ has suffered and died with Him. The attitude of the surrendered Christian should be that of the one who rejects and rebukes the attacks of the world and the desires of the flesh. They seek to do the Will of God, only! As a soldier, you train your mind and your body to think and act as a soldier. Their mind and body are transformed to focus their life for the service of their country. Christ calls us to transform our minds and body for service in the same way to the Father. There must be spiritual death for the mind and heart to be transformed into the pure mind and heart that Christ is seeking to serve in His army. Christ died a spiritual and physical death so that all humanity shall have the opportunity to live and serve God.

PURE IN HEART:
STRENGTHENED AND RENEWED BY THE HOLY SPIRIT

Create in me a clean heart, O God,
And renew a steadfast spirit within me.   (Psalm 51:10)

Understanding the concept of the pure heart can only be seen in relation to the work of the Holy Spirit. The heart of a true servant of Christ is found as a clean heart. This is not only in thought but in their deeds. The Psalm of David shows the desire of a person down to the depths of their soul. They want nothing else but to have a heart and spirit worthy of standing before God without reservation or regret. Can we, as Christians, say that statement truthfully and with complete honesty?

Look deep into the soul of every Believer. There are other things that tend to fall into their path on a day to day basis that can cause them to stumble. There is not one Christian living today that can make that statement honestly. But, thanks be to God! He wants to be the object of your desire. He wants you to go back to your first love. Live each day falling in love with Jesus and experiencing the relationship as new as the previous day is what He desires. When Jesus told John in the vision of Revelation to tell the church at Ephesus that they have lost their first love and that they have forgotten what it was like to be in love with Jesus, it turned the mirror back on every Christian. The people in the Ephesian church were doing everything right, except what was important to God.

In Luke Chapter 10:38-41, Jesus illustrates the difference between a person who is totally focused and has a pure heart and one who is committed to service and forgets about the love of Christ. He said,

> *"Now it happened as they went that He entered a certain village; and a certain woman named Martha welcomed Him into her house. And she had a sister called Mary, who also sat at Jesus' feet and heard His word. But Martha was distracted with much serving, and she approached Him and said, "Lord, do You not care that my sister has left me to serve alone? Therefore, tell her to help me."*

And Jesus answered and said to her, "Martha, Martha, you are worried and troubled about many things." (Luke 10:38-41)

Mary's heart was pure and open to every word that came forth from the mouth of Jesus. Martha, had good intentions and a good heart, and she wanted everything perfect for the Lord Jesus. It was not that Jesus did not appreciate all the things she was doing, but that she was ignoring the most important thing and that was to listen to the small still voice of God through His Son Jesus Christ.

It is the condition of a person's heart that tells the story of their life. When the Psalmist says "create in me a clean heart, O God," he has fallen into the traps of the world and needed to be cleansed. The second part is just as telling when he says, "renew a steadfast spirit within me." These statements are examples of complete surrender of heart and soul to the Spirit of God. Mary, in the story from Luke, illustrates this point as well.

He gives power to the weak,
And to those who have no might He increases strength. Even the
youths shall faint and be weary,
And the young men shall utterly fall,
But those who wait on the LORD
Shall renew their strength;
They shall mount up with wings like eagles,
They shall run and not be weary,
They shall walk and not faint. (Isaiah 40:29-31)

The prophet Isaiah led a unique existence as God's messenger. God chose Isaiah, a common person, to do mighty works for His Kingdom. The difference between the "common" Christian, which there are millions of these, and Isaiah is that he surrendered his life and gave it over to the service of God. It was a hard life, true! But God never promised the life you were called to was going to be easy. Humanity, in all aspects and origins of life, has been given the opportunity by God to be among the greatest in all eternity, but we choose to have our mere fifteen minutes or even fifteen years or even fifty years of fame at the cost of our soul. By this stage in the development of the Christian character, there should be some noticeable fruit.

A person who is pure in heart has surrendered their life to the work of the Lord and knows without question that they are a child of God and His Spirit is strengthening and empowering them for His service. Those beautiful words of the prophet Isaiah put into perspective that it is not them that is doing the work of the Kingdom but Christ who lives in them, through the power of the Holy Spirit. A person who is pure in heart has no doubt from where their strength comes and to where they are led. Christ is the Savior and lover of our soul. This is enough to encourage hope in the Christian Believer. A Believer is therefore strengthened by the empowering grace of God through the work of the Holy Spirit.

PURE IN HEART:
ESSENTIAL FOR SPIRITUAL VISION

Jesus answered and said to him, "Most assuredly, I say to you, unless one is born again, he cannot see the kingdom of God."
(John 3:3)

When a person has surrendered themselves over to the service of Christ, their heart has been changed. They are essentially reborn in the eyes of God. The fruit that flows out of that change must reflect an attitude toward life and all that it pertains. It is essential for the Believer to see or even understand the kingdom perspective from God's point of view. One must make a complete reversal of their previous attitude toward people and life.

Jesus, when He made this statement, was speaking with Nicodemus. Nicodemus was a well-respected Pharisee who saw and understood more than the rules dictated on parchment and stone. He saw something different in Jesus and wanted to learn more. For the most part, the religious orders of Jesus' day were very learned in book knowledge, but were dumb when it came to looking at those writings through the eyes and understanding of God. They were traditional in their ways and the way in which they enforced it. Nicodemus was a Pharisee who wanted more from his beliefs. He did not just look at the "what" in a scripture, he looked deeper into the "why" and the "how." Jesus saw this in his heart. He saw that Nicodemus was searching for more and that he was truly determined in his search for the truth.

When he left Jesus that night, Nicodemus was a changed man. Jesus shared with him the complete plan for his life. But, this must first be understood at the point where Nicodemus stood, he was renewed in his heart. The heart life must grow through the power of the Holy Spirit and be cleansed by that power to become pure in heart. The confusion comes when a person is renewed or regenerated by the experience of conversion. But, it is through a life of growing from that seedling into that fruitful and fertile tree that a person can experience life of the person who is pure in heart.

WHERE DO WE GO FROM HERE?

The Believer with a pure heart has their eyes on God and Him alone. The world will not be a distraction. Especially the heart that has been cleansed from sin is aimed at total obedience. The one which allows the Holy Spirit to work a great work within them will truly have a heart that is pure before a Holy God.

A person who has a pure heart is one who is willing to give even his life for the gospel of Christ. Look at the life and ministry of the Apostle Paul. In his letter to the churches of Colossae, Laodicea and the surrounding areas, he encourages them to continue in the word and love to which they had been called. Live the love of Christ!

> *But above all these things put on love, which is the bond of perfection. And let the peace of God rule in your hearts, to which also you were called in one body; and be thankful. Let the word of Christ dwell in you richly in all wisdom, teaching and admonishing one another in psalms and hymns and spiritual songs, singing*

> *with grace in your hearts to the Lord. And whatever you do in*
> *word or deed, do all in the name of the Lord Jesus, giving thanks*
> *to God the Father through Him.*   (Colossians 3:14-17)

Purity in the heart means to have an open heart for obedience to the call of God. The focus of one's life becomes crystal clear for the things of God. The beauty of the creation and glory of God is revealed. Also, the ugliest of the sinful world is made known to the one with a pure heart. When the eyes of your heart are opened by the Holy Spirit, you will see the world in new light through the eyes of God and for His glory.

CLOSING PRAYER:

> *Father in heaven and my Lord and Savior, create in me a clean*
> *and pure heart so that I may serve you in Spirit and in Truth. I pray*
> *that I glorify You with all my heart. Open my eyes that I my see all*
> *that You see that serve in clear obedience to the glory and honor of*
> *the Father and the Son through the power of the Holy Spirit.*
> *In Jesus Name, Amen.*

QUESTIONS FOR DISCUSSION

Pure in Heart Toward God

1. What is your spiritual mission and does it come from a pure heart?

2. What does it mean to be "pure in heart" in relation to death to self in your spiritual growth?

3. Maintaining and growing a pure heart, where should your focus be and what is the source of that growth?

4. Why is a pure heart essential for spiritual vision in life?

8

SHOWING THE PEACE OF CHRIST TO THE LOST

Blessed are the peacemakers,
For they shall be called sons of God. (Matthew 5:9)

The peacemakers in the world are better known as the diplomats. The diplomat then recalls governmental politics which becomes a negative and counterproductive adversary to peace. The term peacemaker tends to be tossed around and twisted by every church and secular agenda. We, as surrendered Christians, should therefore focus on and bring to our understanding the notion of the peace of Christ as the true peace. Those who seek peace for God's sake toward an eternal goal and purpose, they will be called peacemakers. The belief systems and family groups are similar in the way things are balanced. There is always a good and bad, a yin and yang, a male and female. These are opposites that come together to form the whole. There are many more examples in all forms of existence. In the home, there is found one to be the disciplinarian and one to be the peacemaker. When the Spirit of God is at work in your life, there is a peace that passes all understanding. The notion of receiving this peace comes with the understanding that you must share it.

The essential work of Christ in a lost and dying world is that the peace of Christ is spread. The word of God is to be read and the love of God is to be shared. The peacemaker is one who, with great confidence and faith, will stand in the gap and consider the face of adversity and evil and cast it into the sea. It is the peacemakers who are seen by their lifestyles.

The number one fear that strikes a Christian as they grow in character and their relationship with Christ, is the fear of having to stand up and profess. The fear to stand and speak or share their heart. When adversity comes, the natural reaction that is common to all and is said to be found at the core of human nature is called the "Fight or Flight" reaction to a situation. The peacemaker stands between them.

The peacemaker meets a person at the point of vulnerability in their life. They listen to their hurts, their concerns, their venting and frustrations. Peacemakers possess spiritual discernment that is empowered by the Holy Spirit. The Holy Spirit is the only way by which most people stand against situations in their lives. The level of understanding at this point is seen in accordance with the empowerment of the Spirit in a person's life. Confidence and strength are evident, yet a humble and meek spirit is seen to the point that the adversary is brought to a calming position. Understanding the Spirit's role at this point in the life of the Believer is evident in their actions in times of loss. When God sets a hurting person in the path of a Believer, the Holy Spirit encourages and empowers them to be an ambassador of peace for Christ. The role of the Holy Spirit, with the peacemaker, is to be found in their strength, stability, and wisdom.

PEACEMAKERS: GOD'S VESSELS FOR PEACE

Deceit is in the heart of those who devise evil,
But counselors of peace have joy.   (Proverbs 12:20)

The peace that is found in the resting arms of our Savior Jesus Christ is a peace that truly cannot be described by mere words on a page. It is through the actions and way of life of the individual that demonstrates peace. Jesus, during His ministry demonstrated the purest example of what it means to be a peacemaker. The world rejected Him and His teachings, even in the town in which He was raised as a child and teen. What was so awe encompassing about Jesus was when He stood before adversaries such as demons and even the devil, Satan, himself. A person could just look in the eyes of Jesus and the Holy Spirit that was in Him made a connection. That connection would bring about a peace that passes all understanding and comfort in times of turmoil to an individual who was lost but eagerly seeking redemption. Those who strive to be deliverers of peace are the ones who reflect God's calming wisdom and understanding in times of strife and chaos. God is a God of peace and what He wants is for His creation to be at peace once again.

The role of the Holy Spirit is to bring into the picture the true perception of the Spirit of God through the willing Believer to the one suffering. There is great joy to be found in the life of the Believer who has discovered the peace of Christ through the power of the Holy Spirit and has the willingness to share the peace of Christ with a lost and dying world. Peace is demonstrated as much, if not more, in the actions of the individual versus than in their words. In many churches, they call for a "passing of the peace." This is showing the peace of Christ to one another, within the church building, with a holy hug or handshake. This is all great, but what about those people outside the doors of the church building who are truly struggling, starving for the love and peace of Christ and do not see it or feel it. The Believer is called to pass the peace to those in need of peace, not as a social moment to catch up on the latest gossip in town or even around the church.

The view of many who have been "turned off" by church is that there seems to be more sin *in* the church than outside of it. It seems to be very hard to find true Bible preaching and teaching churches who walk the talk. These rare congregations don't root around in their own hypocrisy, waiting on the next feel good message to justify their sinful weekly activities. But, the righteous Believer who strives for the true peace of God in their life will find it as they become an empowered vessel to be used by God to spread His peace to all mankind.

PEACEMAKERS: STRIVING FOR THE PEACE OF CHRIST

Pursue peace with all people, and holiness, without which
no one will see the Lord: (Hebrews 12:14)

The holy life cannot be possible apart from the empowering work of the Holy Spirit. Living life in general is hard enough living alone. Knowing that God is with you in your everyday life is not only comforting but enormously peaceful by any standard. Those who claim to have life by the horns with money and power have an incredible void in their lives that make them strive for more of the same thing. Power, material wealth, and monetary abundance cannot fill the tremendous hole left in the soul of an individual apart from Christ.

The Atheist says that there is no God. But, philosophically, because they understand and mention the concept idea is proof there is a God. Their god is in other things. How do we understand the peace of God through our Lord and Savior in the power of the Holy Spirit? The world's view of peace is quite possibly between countries, armies or people. The peace that is offered by the grace of God is a peace that cannot be described by human speech or understood by human ears. A person who is a true Believer and lives by faith in Jesus Christ, is one who is continually striving forward toward a goal that is to serve Christ and Him alone. The peace seen at the base of this Believer is evidence of the sanctifying work of Christ in their life. Because they are different, people seeking what they have are drawn to them.

The understanding of the peacemaker can be seen in the lives of various groups of spiritualists. They were called to a life solely dedicated to seeking the true holiness found only in the working power of the Holy Spirit. Beginning in the early 1600's, a group of Lutheran Believers, later to be known as the Pietists, studied the early spiritual teachings of Martin Luther and the early church fathers, mainly the Cappadocian fathers such as Gregory of Nyssa. They chose to focus more on the idea of holiness and spirituality as opposed to formal religious practices of the church of the day. The notion of "rebirth" and the complete reversal of a person's mind set and lifestyle stood juxtaposed to belief found in the church of the time. As in the days of Martin Luther, the institutionalized religious establishment had set a new standard in hypocrisy. The work of the Holy Spirit was primarily a footnote in a long history of footnotes that came with its many wars and political issues. The Pietists and others with similar beliefs were those who stood in the gap for the peace of Christ, many took a stand at great costs. Many Believers gave their lives for the peace they sought so eagerly to achieve.

PEACEMAKERS: SOWERS WHO REAP RIGHTEOUSNESS

But the wisdom that is from above is first pure, then peaceable, gentle, willing to yield, full of mercy and good fruits, without partiality and without hypocrisy. Now the fruit of righteousness is sown in peace by those who make peace. (James 3:17-18)

The road traveled toward sanctification and a life of righteousness is one that is truly narrow with many hills and valleys. But, at the end of the journey, there will be a great reward. The peacemaker, as they grow closer to God, becomes more in tuned with the mission of peace and seeks to sow peace that will grow into righteousness. Jesus set the example for His disciples as He traveled all over Galilee and Judea bringing the message of peace. He never sought to argue or fight with individuals who disagreed with Him, but rather led them to a better understanding of the scriptures and their intended meaning. As with the parable of the sower and the seed, Jesus demonstrated the result of this action. First, the seed that landed on good soil, soil that was receptive to the Word of God, flourished and grew strong. Even more for the one who harvests the product of a successful sowing, the harvester will reap a great harvest when the Holy Spirit prepares the way and does the work of Christ through the individual. The one who sows will most likely never see the result of their labor. For every person who receives Jesus Christ as Lord and Savior, there are probably a minimum of six attempts by people to reach them. Generally, for most people, it is the seventh or eighth contact that finally brings them to an active decision to accept Jesus as their Lord and Savior.

Because of their empathy and approach to people, peacemakers are unique in the way they enter conversations concerning faith. The calming demeanor in which they approach any divine appointment usually sets an individual at ease in an otherwise stressed and awkward series of questions for most people. Usually, a peacemaker has a legitimate reason for the peace in their lives. When the peace of Christ is sown through the work of the Holy Spirit, a harvest of righteousness is seen in the life of the recipient.

The peacemaker seeks after nothing but peace in the spirit for those who struggle with life. There are many aspects of life that are difficult for most individuals to deal with as well as accept. These are the times where Christ leads, through the Holy Spirit, the peacemaker into a situation of chaos to bring calming and peace in a situation. Understanding the responsibility of those who are called upon to be peacemakers will assist them in the overall realization of their growing relationship. It will bring them to an openness to the authority and power given to them by the empowerment of the Holy Spirit. More importantly, a life that is lived in the Spirit and not the flesh.

WHERE DO WE GO FROM HERE?

The peacemaker is the one who, with no concern for their own life, will stand in place of another for the sake of Jesus. Jesus stood for us in eternity when He went to the cross and laid down His life for us. The peacemaker has a love for the lost that is unmatched with any other individuals. The beauty of their presence in times of strife and chaos brings a calming effect to a situation.

The countenance and glory of God is seen, on many occasions, exhibited in the life and actions of the peacemaker. Begin to look deep into your own heart and ask the Holy Spirit to reveal your strengths and weaknesses. Through this practice, you will be able to thoroughly understand and further grow in the power of the Holy

Spirit. The peacemaker is one who is stronger than most because they have overcome the fear of this world and seeks nothing but a peaceful solution to a given problem.

> *Pursue peace with all people, and holiness, without which*
> *no one will see the Lord:* (Hebrews 12:14)

This verse should speak to all those of believe they have a clean path into the peace of God. We need to allow the peace of God to flow through us to a lost and dying world. Do you believe that Christians need to pursue peace not only in their lives but in the lives of all those who seek the Lord Jesus Christ with all their hearts? This is the personal concern that needs to be addressed. You need not pursue the idea of being a peacemaker until there is true peace between you and your Lord and Savior Jesus Christ.

CLOSING PRAYER:

> *O Most gracious heavenly Father, guide my path that I may*
> *pursue peace with all men. Father, may You be glorified and Your*
> *calling on my life not be given in vain. For I seek your peace. The*
> *peace that passes beyond all human understanding for my guidance*
> *and strength. In Jesus' Name, Amen*

QUESTIONS FOR DISCUSSION

God's Peacemakers

1. Who are considered as peacemakers and how does this peace differ from that of the world?

2. How does God bring peace to a chaotic and lost world?

3. How can you effectively strive to achieve the peace of Christ?

4. What is the result of being a sower of peace?

9

LOOKING TO CHRIST IN PHYSICAL PERSECUTION

Blessed are those who are persecuted for righteousness' sake,
for theirs is the kingdom of heaven.   (Matthew 5:10)

Throughout the history of the Christian Church, persecution and ultimately martyrdom had become common place. The greatest prize for the Christian was to die for the sake of the gospel. Jesus Christ suffered and died for us, so the only logical conclusion to the scenario would be that we should pay Him back in like manner. I believe that Jesus Christ suffered and died on that dreadful cross so that we would have life. A Christian is no good to God dead. Granted, in times of persecution, millions of Christians over the centuries have laid down their lives for the sake of the Gospel. But, I am referring to those who go out of their way to be in harm's way, when more lives could benefit from their living witness of the Kingdom than it ever would in their death.

Church history has many people who chose this path to be in the presence of God and out of the torment of the world. Persecution isn't something someone should seek after. But, we need to be prepared to stand strong in the power of the Holy Spirit. The Christian should be a living sacrifice before the Lord and an example to those lost around them.

The Apostle Paul was a prime example of someone persecuted physically, emotionally, and spiritually by his peers, yet he stood strong and continued pressing forward toward the goal of the glory of God. Jesus told His disciples on countless occasions they would suffer because of Him. But, Paul was different. Paul was a person greatly feared and hated by the Christians, followers of the Way as they were called early on. He served his reign of terror on humble Christians for several years. It came to a sudden end when he and his companions were on their way to Damascus. There were reports of some Followers of the Way residing in the city. While on his way, he had a personal encounter with the living Christ, who is Jesus.

Saul was then led into the city by his companions where the Lord called on a faithful follower named Ananias. The Lord got Ananias' attention when He said that he was to go to the house where Saul of Tarsus was staying. If anything, he was in fear for his life, but he was empowered with the Holy Spirit. Through the Holy Spirit, he went with confidence and walked up to the "destroyer of Christ." Ananias knew without a doubt that the Lord called him for this moment.

> But the Lord said to him, "Go, for he is a chosen vessel of Mine to bear My name before Gentiles, kings, and the children of Israel. For I will show him how many things he must suffer for My name's sake." (Acts 9:15-16)

This statement of the Lord would truly play out in the life of the newly converted Paul. Out of all those recorded in the New Testament, apart from Jesus Himself, Paul was physically persecuted more than any one person. He was beaten, flogged, stoned (on several occasions), left for dead, imprisoned and during the entire time, he never wavered from his called for the gospel of Christ. In the end, he would be crucified at the hand of Emperor Nero around 64 A.D. (as most accounts describe it).

Understanding persecution in today's terms is much the same as it was in the day of Paul. You can find yourself in a situation of physical persecution. There are those today, in certain countries, who have died for the faith. The most telling are those in the United States today who had died for the faith, because they would not renounce Jesus Christ. The incident at Columbine for example. Americans tend to separate themselves from the truth that looms before them until it looks them in the face. The Christians who are called to the various missions of the world suffer for the cause of Christ, even today, as they proclaim the truth of the gospel. What gives a person the strength to stand against the powers of the evil in the world? The Holy Spirit that dwells and empowers those who are called children of God. Paul knew without a doubt that he had a new mission, a true mission, that he would be empowered to endure until his execution for the sake of the gospel of Christ.

PERSECUTED: DYING FOR CHRIST

For we who live are always delivered to death for Jesus' sake,
that the life of Jesus also may be manifested in our mortal flesh.
(2 Corinthians 4:11)

The Christian should believe that God is forever at work through the Holy Spirit in the life of those who love Him by this stage of growth. It becomes the element that drives the person to stand in the face of evil with confidence and faith. There are times in the life of humans, because of our human nature, that arrogance and pride play a key role in the fall from grace. When the frail human psyche faces impending death, they begin to lose the will to live. But, when a person who has been born into the family of God, through the power of the Holy Spirit, stares into the face of death, the spirit of the person rejoices. Their hope comes because they will dwell in the presence of their Creator. The difference in the attitude and focus of the born-again Christian becomes truly evident.

Let us look at the disciple Stephen in Acts Chapter six. The writer of Acts tells us, from the start, that Stephen was a man who was full of the Holy Spirit and full of faith. If there was any man who gave himself, even unto death, for the sake of the gospel of Christ, it was Stephen. He had no regard for his own life but gave for the sake of others without any reservations. His martyrdom set in motion the spread of Christianity into all the world. It also was the point at which the early establishments of the church began to be sown. At this point, because of the persecution that followed Stephen's death, Christians began to run in fear. Many Christians ran, in fear for their lives, to far parts of the empire to be able to worship the Lord Jesus Christ.

The Apostle Paul, in his letter to the Christians in Rome, wrote a treatise that established the whole of the plan of salvation. In the letter to the Roman churches, he not only indicates the plan of salvation, but he also reveals the struggles that are evident while trying to live the righteous Christian life. Paul knew as well as anyone the difficulties of being a child of God in a lost and evil world. He writes in Chapter eight that there is hope even in this life through our Lord and Savior Jesus Christ as children of the living God.

> *The Spirit Himself bears witness with our spirit that we are children of God, and if children, then heirs—heirs of God and joint heirs with Christ, if indeed we suffer with Him, that we may also be glorified together.*   (Romans 8:16-17)

Paul had been persecuted to the point of death on several occasions, but he remained strong, steadfast and focus on the goal to which he desired to achieve with all his heart. The Saul (Paul), who was a Pharisee among Pharisees, turned away completely and went from persecuting Christians for God to *being* persecuted for the sake of Jesus Christ. Until his death at the hand of the Emperor Nero, Paul stayed the course that was set before him to serve and love Christ with all his heart, mind, soul and strength. Even when his body had been nearly destroyed, his soul and heart remained true and steadfast. It is only through the power and ministry of the Holy Spirit in the lives of individuals like Paul that the gospel of God's Grace will spread into all the world.

PERSECUTED: SUFFERING FOR BEING A CHRISTIAN

> *Beloved, do not think it strange concerning the fiery trial which is to try you, as though some strange thing happened to you;*

> *but rejoice to the extent that you partake of Christ's sufferings, that when His glory is revealed, you may also be glad with exceeding joy.* (1 Peter 4:12-13)

The fear of death is the fear most common to the human mind. The one thing that Christians have to their advantage over those of the world is that death for them has been conquered. There is a hope beyond death that the world does not know or understand. The Holy Spirit is at work in the Christian who eagerly seeks after the face of God to the point that death is not an issue. Jesus Christ, following His death, descended into hell and conquered death and sin in order that those who truly seek after Him will be given the hope of eternal life. The Christian, no matter how close to the Lord, will suffer for the sake of the gospel of Christ. The difference between this idea and the world's notion is that the Holy Spirit is the Comforter and Guide. The Holy Spirit also empowers and strengthens the individual for service to the Lord. As a person grows closer to a real relationship with Jesus Christ, the power that is the Holy Spirit, assists them in the development of their faith. This is needed to survive any attacks from the evil one.

There are many who have stood to face death in the power of the Holy Spirit to enter martyrdom as an eternal child of God. The crown of glory is given to those who stand and face what the evil one throws against them. Jesus said that you will suffer and some even to the death. (For example, Stephen was the first documented martyrdom following the death of Jesus.(Acts 6:8-7:60) He saw the heavens open and the Son of God seated at the right hand of God. He willingly gave his life for the gospel of Christ. As a result, word spread throughout the Roman Empire and Christianity went global. James the Apostle, brother of John, was martyred for his stance on the gospel (Acts 12:1-3). Herod Agrippa I beheaded him to send a message to the church in Jerusalem. Another example of a willing martyrdom was that of Polycarp, a disciple of the Apostle John. Polycarp had served the Lord for over eighty-six years and said to the proconsul, "God's will be done." They burned him at the stake and he willingly stood and prayed as the fire consumed him. He would not profess the Emperor as god, so he was executed because he would not waiver and renounce his Lord. (Eusebius: The History of the Church)

God created us to worship, love, and serve Him. If a person chooses to put themselves in harm's way to be martyred for the faith, it is because of their hope for the glory of the Father and the Son and eternal life. It is not for notoriety, but for Christ that these and many others were willing to sacrifice themselves for the Jesus' sake and the gospel. He said to "Go! Make disciples of all the nations!" A person who is preoccupied with being martyred for the faith seems to be more self-serving and has lost focus and the true meaning of what it means to be martyred for your faith. (pp. 198-199)

When you seek out death, you are basically indirectly committing suicide. This goes against all that God desires for His people to do. If He called everyone to commit suicide so that they could be with Him, that would be one thing. But, there is a direct command in the ten commandments that plainly states "Thou shalt not kill!" When a person kills themselves, they are just as guilty of murder as if they had killed another person. The idea of martyrdom introduces the notion of dying, out of your control, for the sake of the gospel. When Stephen was stoned to death by the Sanhedrin, he spoke in the power of the Holy Spirit in defense of the Gospel of Christ. That is what it means to die for Christ!

Persecuted: Finding Life amid Loss

He who finds his life will lose it, and he who loses his life for
My sake will find it.   (Matthew 10:39)

Following Jesus Christ and being a true disciple is not an easy and carefree life. Jesus told His disciples that they would suffer for His name sake. Many died gruesome deaths because of their faith. When a person comes into a relationship with Jesus Christ, they are a new creation. The old person is dead and a new person is formed in its place. This means that when a person has truly surrendered their life to God they have completely transformed their mind and all their associations. Because of this total reversal of thought, the growth process begins to "reboot new programming" into the mind.

As the mind focuses more and more on the things of God, the heart and spirit grows closer as well. This causes the person to trust in faith that Christ is with them, regardless of the outcome. Life or death, they know that the will of God is going to be accomplished.

The ability to accept life or death in the name of Jesus Christ is a total act of self-denial. When Peter stepped out of the boat on the Sea of Galilee to walk to the Lord on the water, it was not until he took his eyes *off* the Lord and focused on his surroundings that he began to be overcome by the seas. It is the person who is unquestionably focused on Jesus in all things, regardless of the situation, that they will follow Jesus to the death and follow through with it. Whoever surrenders their life totally to the worship and service of the Lord Jesus Christ will not find that their lives are a loss, but to the contrary, not even death will separate them from the unconditional love of God. One sure thing must be understood that, being sinful creatures, it is a struggle to act in total obedience to the will of God. It is only through the power and authority of the Holy Spirit that the Believer can stand face to face with death, even unexpectedly, confidently looking to the eternal hope promised.

WHERE DO WE GO FROM HERE?

The concept of persecution is a difficult one to truly understand if you have not experienced it yourself. The thoughtful consideration of physical torture and death for the American Christian is, for the most part, inconceivable. American Christians today are oblivious to the sufferings of those in other countries. Therefore, they cannot sympathize with their everyday struggle. What would we do if we are faced with war in our backyard again? How would history play out in a country with millions of "born-again Christians?"

Who shall separate us from the love of Christ? Shall tribula-
tion, or distress, or persecution, or famine, or nakedness, or peril,
or sword? As it is written: "For Your sake we are killed all day
long; We are accounted as sheep for the slaughter." Yet in all these
things we are more than conquerors through Him who loved us.

(Romans 8:35-37)

When you give your life completely over to the Lord Jesus
Christ, you are surrendering and trusting to the Will of God. In
times of physical suffering and persecution, the Holy Spirit is given
as a source of comfort and strength. Give Him the glory and the
authority to fully guide you through the times of pain and suffering
in Jesus name. Because great is your reward as you endure for Jesus'
sake. Focus on Him and allow the Holy Spirit to be your eternal
source of comfort and strength.

CLOSING PRAYER:

Heavenly Father, most gracious Lord and savior, I seek your
strength in my times of weakness. I seek your comfort in my deepest
struggles. I pray for those who strive to destroy the body, but Lord, I
pray You strengthen my spirit that I may endure all things the enemy
uses to destroy me. In Jesus' Name, Amen.

QUESTIONS FOR DISCUSSION

Enduring Persecution for Christ's Sake

1. What should be our focus in times of physical persecution?

2. Where should the Christian find strength in the attacks of
    the enemy?

3. Did Jesus tell you or where have you read in scripture that the
    Christian life is an easy one? Why?

4. Where do we find hope within loss?

10

FACING THE GIANTS FOR THE SAKE OF CHRIST

Blessed are you when they revile and persecute you, and say all kinds of evil against you falsely
for My sake. (Matthew 5:11)

The glory of the Father is shown through the works of the Holy Spirit. He is at work in the individual Believer who acknowledges and lives a life committed solely to Jesus Christ His Son. This life is not a perfect one because it is one filled with sin encounters and the evil present in an otherwise good and perfect world. The Holy Spirit is given to God's people as the ever-present person of Jesus Christ at work within their lives to guide and comfort.

The need for a comforter becomes clear when a person comes into a relationship with Jesus Christ and receives the Holy Spirit. The world and the evil within it is more and more evident. Therefore, the openness a person seems to exhibit brings clarity in their mind, heart, and spirit. Then, they can focus on the needs of the individual apart or even instead of their own needs. At this level of growth in the process toward spiritual sanctification, the Believer becomes truly aware of their spiritual surroundings. They can stand strong against the slander and false accusations that are thrown against them. At this point, the person will pray for that individual, despite the degree of slanderous things said to them or about them. As in the past, the true Believer and follower of Christ is more willing to face death for the sake of Christ rather than face slander and false accusations against them.

Facing the giants in your life is the most difficult aspect of the Christian walk to have to encounter. This is because you must truly face them and you cannot just walk away. Every day of your life you are reminded by the world of your insignificance in accordance with the world's standards.

FACING THE GIANTS: THE STRUGGLE FROM WITHIN

When He had called all the multitude to Himself, He said to them, "Hear Me, everyone, and understand: There is nothing that enters a man from outside which can defile him; but the things which come out of him, those are the things that defile a man. If anyone has ears to hear, let him hear!" (Mark 7:14-16)

The struggle within a person is what hinders their growth spiritually. Every moment of every day an individual must make decisions based on their experiences, lifestyle, and understanding. This forms their character and the processes by which they must make informed decisions. The Holy Spirit in the life of the true Believer gives a more informed knowledge for interacting with the world around them. The tendency is to conform and not be transformed by the renewing of their mind. The Apostle Paul, in his letter to the Roman church, spoke directly to this very real struggle. But, this dictates the way the person reacts to every situation in any given moment. When someone makes attempts to slander or speak falsely against you, as Christians, Jesus tells you to turn the other cheek or even pray for them.

The last thing, in the worldly view of understanding, a person wants to do is to walk away or especially pray for them. But, Jesus tells us to love one another as He has loved us, this includes our enemies and those who come against us to destroy us. The Holy Spirit is given to every Believer to bring comfort and strength. He is given to assist the Believer in making informed and Godly decisions based on the unconditional love that God has for us. The struggle within, by all accounts, through the power and work of the Holy Spirit, should be a mute topic and the Believer must move on and grow. The reality is that everyone battles with sin and its effects every day of their life. The solution is to focus solely on Christ and His love. The desire is to share that love with others, even those who attempt to defame and destroy us.

> *When He had entered a house away from the crowd, His disciples asked Him concerning the parable. So He said to them, "Are you thus without understanding also? Do you not perceive that whatever enters a man from outside cannot defile him, because it does not enter his heart but his stomach, and is eliminated, thus purifying all foods?"* (Mark 7:17-19)

Are Christians so dense that they do not see the forest for the trees? Maybe, or possibly they are blinded by worldly desires and knowledge. Whatever the case, it becomes a question of can the Christian fully surrender and lay their burdens at the foot of the cross and abandon the world and its deceptions. So, as the Christian stands firm in the line of attacks, they need to remember that Jesus suffered far more than they would ever imagine suffering for a greater purpose, their eternal soul. Jesus goes on to say;

> *"What comes out of a man, that defiles a man. For from within, out of the heart of men, proceed evil thoughts, adulteries, fornications, murders, thefts, covetousness, wickedness, deceit, lewdness, an evil eye, blasphemy, pride, foolishness. All these evil things come from within and defile a man."* (Mark 7:20-23)

When a person is attacked, it is the time of most vulnerability and they become as an animal backed into a corner. They tend to attack out of self-defense. But, as we have learned from Jesus Himself, that ignorance of the situation and those involved is no excuse. Sharing God's love and praying for those who come against you for the sake of the gospel of Christ is at the center of the call. Therefore, it must be understood that when the one who professes Jesus Christ, especially before their enemies, even amid being persecuted, the Holy Spirit is the one who goes before them. He prepares the way and protects them from the fiery darts and arrows that the evil one fires at them. Even though God allowed Satan to attack Job in everything, including material possessions and family, Job remained faithful. And even though God allowed Satan to attack Job's body to the point of death, Job did sin against God. He stayed faithful. Most people, most Christians, would have turned and ran full stride away from God instead of into His loving embrace.

The tongue, according the epistle of James, is the sharpest and deadliest tool at our disposal. It can also be the best blessing in the spread of the gospel of Jesus Christ and to share a comforting word with someone hurting, unlike those friends of Job who thought they were giving wise counsel.

FACING THE GIANTS: ETERNAL FORGIVENESS

For if you forgive men their trespasses, your heavenly Father will also forgive you. But if you do not forgive men their trespasses, neither will your Father forgive your trespasses.
(Matthew 6:14-15)

When people come against you to destroy your life and your ministry, the "knee jerk" reaction is to reciprocate by facing them down in the same manner. We do this because of the sinful nature that rests deep within the human heart. It is a reaction based on a defense mechanism established because of environmental, emotional, and experiential encounters in the life of the individual. God knows all your junk, even the stuff you don't want Him to know. What you try to keep from God is the very things that should be given to Him. Because they are probably those hurting and damaging aspects that are slowly and systematically destroying your life and ministry. Eternal forgiveness is only given by God the Father, through the Son, by means of the Holy Spirit. When people speak against someone, it is usually due to ignorance or a sense of inferiority.

Understanding the "who" many times helps to understand the "why" in any given situation. "Why am I being attacked? Why is life so frustrating and difficult? Why do I seem to be the target of such terrible abuse, emotionally, mentally, and verbally?" The difference between human forgiveness and divine forgiveness is found in the Greek understanding of "love." The Greeks were very concise with their defining of terms. Every time Jesus referred to the love of the Father or His love for His people, the term *agape* was used. Other incidences when referring to an understanding of love, the term was *philos*, brotherly love, or *eros*, lustful or sexually immoral love. Jesus calls all who believe in Him to a life of *agape* or unconditional love. The type of love that a person, who is committed and focused solely on Jesus Christ and Him alone, can experience and share with others. Jesus said "Love one another as I have loved you." He raised the disciples from friends, to brothers, to true heirs to the promise. Forgiveness rooted in God's *agape* love stands as the foundation for a person's life in Christ.

> *"Either make the tree good and its fruit good, or else make the tree bad and its fruit bad; for a tree is known by its fruit. Brood of vipers! How can you, being evil, speak good things? For out of the abundance of the heart the mouth speaks. A good man out of the good treasure of his heart brings forth good things, and an evil man out of the evil treasure brings forth evil things. But I say to you that for every idle word men may speak, they will give account of it in the day of judgment. For by your words you will be justified, and by your words you will be condemned."* (Matthew 12:33-37)

The words spoken in jest or in anger or even in a twisted form of love can either build up or destroy an individual. Trying to relate to a person and empathize with them on their level of understanding is virtually impossible without the preparation, guidance, and authority of the Holy Spirit. Most Christians tend to step out on their own without adequate time with the Lord. When you act out of the flesh and not of the Spirit, the result can be more damaging than comforting.

The Holy Spirit was sent to be the Comforter. The one who is sent by God to "comfort." He knows more and has much more experience with comfort than any human being. Human beings, in the flesh, tend to assume too much when it comes to comfort and consoling. They tend to take the "insert foot in mouth" method or approach to comforting people. If they would rely on the Holy Spirit for guidance and strength, they would never go wrong. Because of this, they become fuel to the problem and not a solid solution. Christians need to pray and seek the face of God before speaking. They have the upper hand and understanding on how to speak and share with others. Allow the Holy Spirit to work through you and don't be led by your own assumptions and carnal understandings because you will answer for those words and actions in the end.

WHERE DO WE GO FROM HERE?

The human natural reaction to slander and those who attempt to destroy our reputation is retaliation. The worst part of psychological and emotional persecution is that it goes much deeper than any knife and bullet. Words penetrate even to the soul and spirit of the individual. This is especially true with Christians.

People in the world are under the false impression that Christians are somehow immune and protected. If anything, Christians are damaged more because they believe they are protected from these attacks and they drop their guard, even in church. In the world, they are somewhat guarded and almost expect it to a degree. But, in the church, they tend to love and trust those with whom they worship. We need to consider the words of Jesus;

> *Rejoice and be exceedingly glad, for great is your reward in heaven, for so they persecuted the prophets who were before you.*
> (Matthew 5:12)

> *If you are reproached for the name of Christ, blessed are you, for the Spirit of glory and of God rests on you.* (1 Peter 4:14)

Jesus has called for us to pray for our enemies. We are to be a light in a world of darkness and chaos. If anyone seeks to destroy your reputation or even your testimony, you and the Lord know the truth. He will honor and reward those who speak and live in His truth. It makes no difference how much those around us try to break us down, Jesus through the power of the Holy Spirit will lift us up and deliver us from the hands of our enemies. So, pray and do not curse, but pray and let the Holy Spirit work in the lives of those who seek our destruction.

CLOSING PRAYER:

Heavenly Father, keep me focused on You and Your glory. May You help me face the giants in my life. Lord, strengthen me that I may conquer my giants with a clean heart. Lord, deliver me from my enemies and have mercy on those whom You will have mercy. In Jesus' Name, Amen.

QUESTIONS FOR DISCUSSION

Facing Your Giants for God's Glory

1. What Giants are you facing in life? How will you stand up to them?

2. Where are the greatest struggles that you face in your life? From outside or from within?

3. Are you willing to forgive those who are considered as your enemies?

4. Even though we may forgive, does the fruit evidenced in everyday life reflect that forgiveness?

11

THE HOLY SPIRIT AND
THE UNIFIED BODY OF CHRIST

Endeavoring to keep the unity of the Spirit in the bond of
peace.   (Ephesians 4:3)

The unified Body of Believers is the strongest defense against the attacks of the evil one. Throughout scripture, God told His people that they should be one with one another and especially with Him. The understanding of a unified Body of Believers is best demonstrated through the teachings of Paul. He uses the analogy of the human body, and all its functions, to show the complexity, but very simple functions, of the body as it continues together as a single unit. Each member of the Body has a specific ministry strength. But, the key element to the effectiveness of the Body is through the Blood that flows in it. The Blood, for the Believer, is that which was shed on the Cross of Calvary for the sins of the whole world. This Blood, poured out onto the earth, was also poured out on all who believe.

The Spirit of Christ was given through the Blood. Therefore, the unifying factor that binds all Believers as the Body of Christ is that same Holy Spirit, the Spirit of the Living God, the Spirit of Christ. The apostle Paul goes on to say in verses four through six of Chapter 4 of his letter to the Ephesian Church that:

> *"There is one body and one Spirit, just as you were called in*
> *one hope of your calling; one Lord, one faith, one baptism; one*

*God and Father of all, who is above all, and through all, and in
you all."*

The beginning verses of this chapter of Ephesians brings forth
the purest idea of the relationship between the Believer, the Father,
and the Body of Christ. This is the "oneness" also seen in the Trinity. Through this oneness, whether in adversity and oppression or
in plenty and happiness, there is only one God, one Son, and one
Holy Spirit that completes the work done in the life of the Believer.

THE HOLY SPIRIT AND THE CHURCH:
LEADS INTO ALL TRUTH

*However, when He, the Spirit of truth, has come, He will
guide you into all truth; for He will not speak on His own authority, but whatever He hears He will speak; and He will tell you
things to come.*   (John 16:13)

The beauty of living for God through Jesus Christ is that we
have a guide or one who does lead us. As the Believer, who has
grown in their walk with the Lord, they begin to rely on the Holy
Spirit for everything. They have begun to become more aware of
the Lord's presence and teachings as an integral part of their lives.
Looking back at the previous chapters, seeing to what lengths one
had traveled, you then begin to understand the Truth of God as it
was and is spoken. Jesus Christ becomes just as real to you as He
was to the disciples two thousand years ago. Before the Holy Spirit
carried you on the journey of a living relationship with Jesus Christ,
you were unable to understand and especially receive all that God
had in store for your life.

The individual Believer, who receives the teachings and leadership of the Holy Spirit, is one who truly "knows" without a shadow
of a doubt that they are a child of God. They have a place with the
Father in heaven. The one who opens themselves up to the work of
the Holy Spirit has opened themselves to the Truth of God.

People on different levels of belief wonder why God does not manifest Himself in mighty ways like He did in the Old Testament. The questions are raised concerning miracles and wonders. When Jesus was present with the people of ancient Judea and Galilee, the big concern was with miracles and wanting Him to show them a sign. Jesus as a leader taught that the truth people seek was to be found in their faith. When Jesus healed someone, or cast out demons or whatever He did, He told His disciples, or the person the miracle was performed on, that it was their faith that healed them. There is your sign and wonder. Jesus taught that if the Believer would just have the faith as small as the littlest seed, a mustard seed, they could move mountains.

Modern day evangelists and healers do the song and dance, but the result rests in power of the Holy Spirit and the faith of the individual. Nothing has changed since the foundation of the world. There is a belief in modern day Christianity that a church must have someone else to be the leader in a church. Remember that God gave the Israelites opportunity to let Him be the leader of His people. They refused Him. He gave them anointed Judges to rule in times of crisis. They began to rely on them and not on God. He then gave them Kings to rule as godly representatives of God with all the bells and whistles. They were human and their human sinful nature had proven to be their downfall. God then raised the standard and gave Himself in His Son to finally show them the error of their ways and lead them into a true, personal relationship with Him. They rejected Him. Then, He gave the opportunity for all of humanity to have a personal and most intimate relationship with Him. God sent His Spirit to live in them to lead those who believe into a spiritual, righteous life with Christ.

People, throughout history, sought after the power through humanity to show their independence apart from anyone or anything. They sought for a physical person who is mighty and powerful and perfect per the world's standards to lead them and to rule as their king forever and ever. God offered Himself, but they rejected Him. There is no one person in all of humanity that has or even will rule as God rules. The true miracle is found in the fact that God has selected, as His ultimate act of mercy, to give His Holy Spirit to be within all who believe in Him and choose to worship Him.

THE HOLY SPIRIT AND THE CHURCH: LEADS BELIEVERS ON THEIR PATHS

While Peter thought about the vision, the Spirit said to him,
"Behold, three men are seeking you. Arise therefore, go down and
go with them, doubting nothing; for I have sent them."

(Acts 10:19-20)

The guidance of the Holy Spirit depends on the receptiveness of the one to whom He speaks. Many people are called by God to serve in a task, even today. But, a weak faith becomes the basis for a weak foundation for the Holy Spirit to build upon in the life of the individual. Peter was still quite immature in his new Holy Spirit empowered faith. Despite the previous three years that he had spent every moment of everyday with Jesus. Despite that Peter was one of his best and most devoted disciples, he still had much to learn about God's grace and the work of the Holy Spirit. He did not truly come to an understanding of the power of the Spirit of God until it was poured out onto him and the others in the upper room.

In this place in the life of Peter, he thought that he knew the ministry God had given him. But, the power of the Holy Spirit and the ministry of God was far larger than he had ever imagined. The moment he was obedient to the leading of the Holy Spirit and the call of God, his life and spiritual understanding would be changed forever. He went the next day with the men, that were sent, to Caesarea and to the house of the centurion named Cornelius. On that day, through the power of the Holy Spirit, all his household and those within the community believed and were baptized with the Holy Spirit and water. Through his obedience to the Spirit of God, he realized that even the Gentiles were given the right to become children of God.

Peter was raised a devout Jew. He had gone far beyond his formal belief system of Judaism and began to acquire an understanding of God that no one else could, apart from the work and revelation of the God's Spirit or Holy Spirit. Following the servant of Cornelius to Caesarea was a true act of faith and openness to the Spirit of God. This was not only the defining moment for the church universally, but for Peter as a Jewish Christian. The Gentiles were heathens and barbarians in the eyes of the Jewish people. For Peter to be called to the Gentiles as a ministry, this was a new understanding for him because of his focus on the lost people of Israel.

THE HOLY SPIRIT AND THE CHURCH: DIRECTS IN THE SELECTION OF HOLY LEADERS

As they ministered to the Lord and fasted, the Holy Spirit said, "Now separate to Me Barnabas and Saul for the work to which I have called them." (Acts 13:2)

When people are totally committed to the work of Jesus Christ, they see Him and Him alone. Their worship is done with great abandonment to themselves and all things that would be a distraction. They truly fast as an example of being a living sacrifice before God as His servants. In the early Christian church, leaders were selected through a full reliance of the Spirit of God by prayer, worship, and fasting as the way of opening themselves to God and to be guided to the right selection.

Modern churches have lost the desire to be living sacrifices and totally abandon themselves to the guidance of Jesus Christ through the empowerment of the Holy Spirit in any decisions concerning church affairs. Churches, for the most part, are committed to the "church's business" and not about God's mission and vision. As a person who has served on church administrative boards and chaired countless committees, I have seen the decline in the strength of the church because of the lack of the empowering strength of the Holy Spirit evident within its membership. The lack of Biblical teaching, preaching and acceptance of the Spirit of God within the assembly of Believers. This has allowed human nature to enter in and the evil one to land a foot-hold on God's people. For the people of God to truly be His people, they must accept His Spirit as they have received Him. The first century church relied on the Spirit of God to guide the church in its business and in choosing the Godly leaders that will lead in the power of that Spirit.

> *Then the twelve summoned the multitude of the disciples and said, "It is not desirable that we should leave the word of God and serve tables. Therefore, brethren, seek out from among you seven men of good reputation, full of the Holy Spirit and wisdom, whom we may appoint over this business; but we will give ourselves continually to prayer and to the ministry of the word." (Acts 6:2-4)*

The selection of the seven to serve as leaders within the church was set firmly in place. The idea of servanthood within the church is not a new concept, but those within mainline churches seem to view it that way. When the Holy Spirit works within the individual Believer, the power of God becomes evident and the glory of God is set as a standard that cannot be matched in the world. When we look back to Moses, his father-in-law Jethro was used by God to guide him to better govern the Israelites. He told him to select those from the clans and tribes that are led by God and full of wisdom, as Godly leaders, to care for the small issues. He instructed him to do this so he could deal more effectively with the larger issues that would affect the nation before God.

When a church fully relies on the Holy Spirit for guidance and leadership, then they will exhibit God's power and authority. Standing firm before the enemies of the Lord Jesus Christ is the purpose for congregational gatherings. We must assemble ourselves together because we are stronger in numbers than when we are alone.

WHERE DO WE GO FROM HERE?

The idea of strength in numbers is literally the truth. The Body of Christ is, as Paul describes, a body with many parts and with one function. This Body, even though it has many members, must work in unity together toward a single end and goal. Jesus and His purpose is the goal.

We have looked thoroughly at the character and called purpose of a true follower of Jesus Christ. Also, the important role of the Holy Spirit in the process of growth in the character and life of the Believer. As you begin to fully walk in the marvelous light of the Holy Spirit, allow the that same Spirit to reign and work in the church and the community.

> *So continuing daily with one accord in the temple, and breaking bread from house to house, they ate their food with gladness and simplicity of heart, praising God and having favor with all the people. And the Lord added to the church daily those who were being saved.* (Acts 2:46-47)

All members of the Body of Christ must live out the greatest commandments. "Love the Lord your God with all your heart, mind, soul, and strength" and "Love one another as Christ loves us." These must be the standards by which the Christian agrees upon to live in harmony with one another and to serve and worship the Lord in Spirit and in Truth. The church will flourish and grow only when they learn to rely on the Holy Spirit and not their own power for guidance and strength.

CLOSING PRAYER:

> *Most gracious heavenly Father I seek your guidance and wisdom to be the Body of Christ You want us to become. It is to Your glory and per Your Will, Lord, that I seek wisdom to lead Your people to become the people who You have called to be the Bride of Christ. In Jesus' Name, Amen.*

QUESTIONS FOR DISCUSSION

The Unified Body of Christ

1. What is the unifying component that must be present in the Body of Christ?

2. If the Spirit of the Truth is present and active in the church today, why is it so segregated in its focus?

3. When the church as the Body of Christ is one in the Holy Spirit, it is single mind in one direction, then why is this mask so in the church?

4. Just as the early church, from the early Apostles forward, selected leaders, is it not the responsibility of the church today to do the same thing? How does your church select leaders?

12

LIVING AS CHILDREN OF THE LIVING GOD

Therefore, be imitators of God as dear children. And walk in love, as Christ also has loved us and given Himself for us, an offering and a sacrifice to God for a sweet-smelling aroma.
(Ephesians 5:1-2)

The desire to live for God, by this time, can be at times overwhelming and exciting. This is when the Christian has truly grown in strength and power through the power of the Holy Spirit. The knowledge and understanding of the one true God brings with it total love, respect, and commitment to the ministry and work of Christ in a lost and dying world. When Jesus called His disciples at the beginning of His earthly ministry, He gave them a mandate to follow for them to live as children of the living God. The "Beatitudes" were to become the foundation for all the teachings and life demonstrations throughout His entire ministry. They laid the ground work for the ability of sinful humanity to have an intimate and growing relationship with the living God of the universe. Everything, including the death and resurrection of Jesus Christ, were all found in the eight basic principles as the first recorded words by Jesus at the beginning of His earthly ministry to His disciples. This is the cornerstone that has been all but forgotten as the core of how God desires for His people, who are called by His name, should grow and live.

CHILDREN OF GOD: LIVING RADIANT LIVES

But we all, with unveiled face, beholding as in a mirror the glory of the Lord, are being transformed into the same image from glory to glory, just as by the Spirit of the Lord.

(2 Corinthians 3:18)

We, as children of God, should live the life that reflects His glory and might. It is only through God's grace and mercy shown in the giving of His Son through the power of His Spirit that a Believer can truly live in the Spirit. The closer someone gets to that intimate relationship, the more open to the work and manifestations of the Spirit that a person grows.

There is an old spiritual song that is popular at church retreats and on mission trips that reflect the oneness Jesus sought for all who believe. In the song, "They will know we are Christians by our love," the common thread that binds all Believers together is love. The "love" cannot be measured by human emotions or desires, but only by the mercy and grace of God through His Holy Spirit.

The result of oneness in the Spirit reflects the Glory of God. As we become true followers and disciples of the living Christ, the presence of Jesus Christ becomes something that sets us apart from the rest of the world. Having a vision for a lost and dying world where people are taking the fast track to eternity in hell, it is the responsibility of the disciple of Jesus to live a life as a radiant beacon of light. They need to be able to see God in us and live in a full relationship with Him through our example.

CHILDREN OF GOD: SPIRITUAL LIGHT FROM THE BELIEVER

You are the light of the world. A city that is set on a hill cannot be hidden. Nor do they light a lamp and put it under a basket, but on a lampstand, and it gives light to all who are in the house. Let your light so shine before men, that they may see your good works and glorify your Father in heaven.

(Matthew 5:14-16)

The children of God are expected by the world to be flawless by their level of standard. But what the world does not realize is that God's standard is much greater. It is based on His eternal mercy and grace. When a person is created in the image of God, the light of that image is part of the spark or flame of life as God breathed into that person. The light of the world was breathed into a soul to create life. As the person grows into a relationship with Jesus Christ, the Light of life grows brighter and becomes more evident. People outside of the faith should see something different and positive in comparison to what is known in the world. The Light is the Light of life and is given to be shared with all people so that God's most precious creation will not perish but come to a relationship with Him. The purpose, as seen in all salvation history, is to reconcile God's people back to a relationship with Him, as it was in the beginning. This Light is the light and life of God the Father, the Son, and the Holy Spirit. The intention is to share it to the glory of the Father in all things.

Light was created to overcome the darkness. The Christian is the Light in the world that is otherwise shrouded in darkness. It only takes a small flicker of light to overwhelm darkness and overtake it. The Believer, who truly follows the teaching of Jesus Christ and yields to the guidance and power of the Holy Spirit, will make a mighty impact in the world for the Kingdom of God. However, small or bright your light may be, God uses everyone to bring His glory into a lost and dying world of darkness. The power and authority of the Holy Spirit is the way the world shall not destroy themselves (John 3:16-17).

CHILDREN OF GOD:
LIVING TEMPLES OF GOD WITHOUT WALLS

I beseech you therefore, brethren, by the mercies of God, that you present your bodies a living sacrifice, holy, acceptable to God, which is your reasonable service. And do not be conformed to this world, but be transformed by the renewing of your mind, that you

may prove what is that good and acceptable and perfect will of
God.   (Romans 12:1-2)

Throughout this study of God's Word, the possibilities of having a lasting and growing relationship with Jesus Christ has been centered on how a Believer understands their connection to the glorious Spirit of the Living God. The Holy Spirit and the relationship with Him is central to the Believer's knowledge and growth in that relationship. God, through His infinite mercy and grace, has paid the ultimate eternal price of the gift of His Son to die in our stead. This was accomplished so all who receive this gift will live in eternity with Him, in beauty and glory.

The gift of the Holy Spirit is given as one merciful act towards His beloved and fallen creation. There is no way that our mere mortal existence will ever measure up to pay back what God has done for us. But, the Apostle Paul says that the best we can offer is our bodies and minds transformed into living sacrifices as a spiritual worship of Him. Humanity does not deserve God's grace and mercy, but He loves us with a true pure love that is reciprocated with our spiritual love and to Him.

Living as sacrifices to God means that Believers are to focus entirely on Jesus Christ alone. The perfect example in this understanding is found in our friend Simon Peter. Peter was the larger than life, boisterous, and determined disciple of Jesus who is our best example among those followers of Jesus as to their humanity. While the rest of the disciples are afraid on the deck of the boat, Peter looked across the sea and recognized the Lord. He did not see an apparition, he saw his Lord walking on the water towards them. When Jesus called him to come out to Him, Peter stepped out of the boat and onto the water. Are we, as Believers in the Lord Jesus Christ, willing to step out in faith regardless the conditions? The tendency of our human nature is focused on our surroundings and the stressful conditions of life and not focused on the Lord and serving Him unconditionally. Where is your faith?

WHERE DO WE GO FROM HERE?

As you stand at the crossroads of your life and life eternal, what are the options in store for you? Are you ready to take hold of the calling for which you have been created, a new creation? The questions we ask ourselves seem pointless considering the unimaginable task that has been set before us. The beauty of it all is that we do not have go through this life alone. God the Father sent His Only Son, who in turn following His ascension, sent His Holy Spirit. With the full power of the God-head, The Trinity, guiding the way, how can we be defeated? If God is for us, who, or even what, can be against us?

Remember, each member of the Trinity made an ultimate sacrifice for your salvation. God the Father gave His Son. God the Son gave His life and God the Holy Spirit gave up His life in the Father and the Son to be in you. And you thought you had a rough day! God the Father, Son and Holy Spirit gave all of Themselves so that you would be reconciled back into a right relationship with Them. So, is our life really that terrible that we cannot love, serve, worship, and obey? It is the *least* we can do! Our best is like dirty rags, but the fact that we have a desire to seek Him, humble ourselves, pray and turn from our wicked ways is a start.

He desires obedience over sacrifice. We are not to lay ourselves on an altar and die bloody. We are to be living sacrifices! How can we further the Kingdom of God dead? His desire is for us to love and serve Him in Spirit and in Truth all the days of our lives. This way more and more people have a chance at salvation, just like we did when we were saved.

> *I beseech you therefore, brethren, by the mercies of God, that you present your bodies a living sacrifice, holy, acceptable to God, which is your reasonable service. And do not be conformed to this world, but be transformed by the renewing of your mind, that you may prove what is that good and acceptable and perfect will of God.* (Romans 12:1-2)

The Will of God is something that we have been searching eagerly for our entire Christian life. The frustrating aspect of all this is that we, during our whole Christian life, have been chasing our tails. We have been thinking that everything was under our sole control and we are set for the pearly gates. Keep in mind that Jesus said that wide is the way that leads to destruction, but narrow is the path that leads to life eternal. It is not as simple as one simple prayer at the altar and your ticket is punched. It is a life! You are a new creation! The old sinful and disgusting human is dead and now you are a new creation in Christ. You are empowered by the Holy Spirit of God. He called you out of the darkness into His wonderful Light. So, now walk and live in it!

CLOSING PRAYER:

O, Most Glorious, Hallowed and heavenly Father. I pray that I shall be a living sacrifice daily for You. Lord, I pray that I live and serve You per Your Will and live from now into eternity every moment of everyday in the light of Your Glory on the path of obedience You have set before me. I shall love, serve, and worship You in all I do and speak. In the Name of the Father, Son, and the Holy Spirit. In Jesus' Name, Amen.

QUESTIONS FOR DISCUSSION

Living as Children of God

1. Considering all that has been understood from this book, how then are we to live as children of God?

2. Do we truly reflect God's glory to people He is calling to repentance?

3. Are we as true Christians of light truly shinning the light of Christ to those walking in darkness or are we also stumbling in the dark?

4. We should not merely contain all who God is but are we temples without walls to share God with those who need Him?

Now, Go and Serve Him in Full Obedience!

ALSO FROM ENERGION PUBLICATIONS

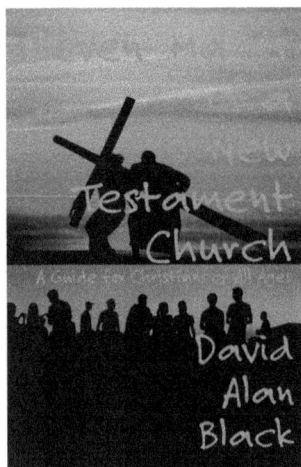

Black's *Seven Marks of a New Testament Church* is a necessary reminder that we are to "do" church on God's terms, not our own.

Dr. Thomas W. Hudgins
Capital Seminary and Graduate School.

Whatever you believe about the Holy Spirit, His gifts and manifestations, you need to read this book.

Rev. Mike Roberts
Retired District Superintendent
United Methodist Church

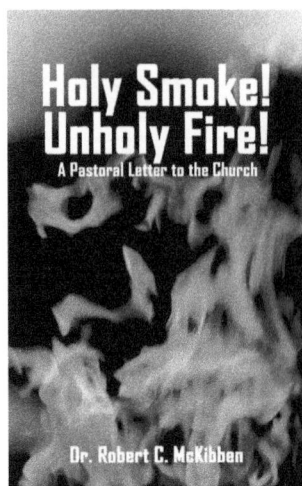

MORE FROM ENERGION PUBLICATIONS

Personal Study

Finding My Way in Christianity	Herold Weiss	$16.99
The Jesus Paradigm	David Alan Black	$17.99
When People Speak for God	Henry Neufeld	$17.99
The Sacred Journey	Chris Surber	$11.99
The Ground of God	Donna Ennis	$12.99

Christian Living

Grief: Finding the Candle of Light	Jody Neufeld	$8.99
Crossing the Street	Robert LaRochelle	$16.99

Bible Study

Learning and Living Scripture	Lentz/Neufeld	$12.99
From Inspiration to Understanding	Edward W. H. Vick	$24.99
Luke: A Participatory Study Guide	Geoffrey Lentz	$8.99
Philippians: A Participatory Study Guide	Bruce Epperly	$9.99
Ephesians: A Participatory Study Guide	Robert D. Cornwall	$9.99

Theology

Creation in Scripture	Herold Weiss	$12.99
Creation: the Christian Doctrine	Edward W. H. Vick	$12.99
The Politics of Witness	Allan R. Bevere	$9.99
Ultimate Allegiance	Robert D. Cornwall	$9.99
History and Christian Faith	Edward W. H. Vick	$9.99
The Church Under the Cross	William Powell Tuck	$11.99
The Journey to the Undiscovered Country	William Powell Tuck	$9.99
Eschatology: A Participatory Study Guide	Edward W. H. Vick	$9.99

Ministry

Clergy Table Talk	Kent Ira Groff	$9.99
In Changing Times	Ron Higdon	$14.99

Generous Quantity Discounts Available
Dealer Inquiries Welcome
Energion Publications — P.O. Box 841
Gonzalez, FL_ 32560
Website: http://energionpubs.com
Phone: (850) 525-3916

www.ingramcontent.com/pod-product-compliance
Lightning Source LLC
LaVergne TN
LVHW011205080426
835508LV00007B/620